Dr. Ruth's
Top 10 Secrets
for Great Sex

Dr. Ruth's
Top 10 Secrets
for Great Sex

*How to Enjoy It, Share It, and
Love It Each and Every Time*

Dr. Ruth K. Westheimer
and Pierre A. Lehu

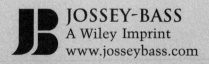

JOSSEY-BASS
A Wiley Imprint
www.josseybass.com

Published by Jossey-Bass
A Wiley Imprint
989 Market Street, San Francisco, CA 94103-1741—www.josseybass.com

Readers should be aware that Internet Web sites offered as citations and/or sources
for further information may have changed or disappeared between the time this was
written and when it is read.

Limit of Liability/Disclaimer of Warranty: While the publisher and author have used
their best efforts in preparing this book, they make no representations or warranties with
respect to the accuracy or completeness of the contents of this book and specifically
disclaim any implied warranties of merchantability or fitness for a particular purpose. No
warranty may be created or extended by sales representatives or written sales materials.
The advice and strategies contained herein may not be suitable for your situation. You
should consult with a professional where appropriate. Neither the publisher nor author
shall be liable for any loss of profit or any other commercial damages, including but not
limited to special, incidental, consequential, or other damages.

Jossey-Bass books and products are available through most bookstores. To
contact Jossey-Bass directly call our Customer Care Department within the U.S.
at 800-956-7739, outside the U.S. at 317-572-3986, or fax 317-572-4002.

Jossey-Bass also publishes its books in a variety of electronic formats. Some content
that appears in print may not be available in electronic books.

Library of Congress Cataloging-in-Publication Data

Westheimer, Ruth K. (Ruth Karola), date.
  Dr. Ruth's top 10 secrets for great sex : how to enjoy it, share it, and love it each and
every time / Ruth K. Westheimer and Pierre A. Lehu.
     p. cm.
  ISBN 978-0-470-42946-4 (pbk.)
  1. Sex instruction. I. Lehu, Pierre A. II. Title. III. Title: Dr. Ruth's top ten secrets for
great sex. IV. Title: Top ten secrets for great sex.
  HQ31.W4963 2009
  613.9'6--dc22

                              2008043469

Printed in the United States of America
FIRST EDITION
PB Printing   10 9 8 7 6 5 4 3 2 1

To all those seeking to improve their love life

I loved you with an eternal love . . .

—Jeremiah 31:3

Contents

Acknowledgments

To the memory of my entire family who perished during the Holocaust. To the memory of my late husband, Fred, who encouraged me in all my endeavors. To my current family: my daughter, Miriam Westheimer, Ed.D.; my son-in-law Joel Einleger, M.B.A.; their children Ari and Leora; my son, Joel Westheimer, Ph.D.; my daughter-in-law Barbara Leckie, Ph.D.; and their children Michal and Benjamin. I have the best grandchildren in the entire world!

Thanks to all the many family members and friends for adding so much to my life. I'd need an entire chapter to list them all but some must be mentioned here: Pierre Lehu and I have now collaborated on a dozen books; he's the best Minister of Communications I could have asked for! Cliff Rubin, my assistant, thanks! Peter Berger, M.D., David Best, David Goslin, Ph.D., Dean Craig Harwood, Steve Kaplan, Ph.D., Bonnie Kaye, Robert Krasner, M.D., Marga and Bill Kunreuther, Dean Stephen Lassonde, Lou Lieberman, Ph.D., and Mary Cuadrado, Ph.D., John and Ginger Lollos, Ambassador and Mrs. Raymond Loretan, Philip Prioleau, M.D., Daniel Schwartz, Amir Shaviv, Betsy Sledge, William Sledge, M.D., Jeff Tabak, Esq., Malcolm Thomson, Markus Wilhelm, Greg Willenborg, Ben Yagoda, and Froma Zeitlin, Ph.D. And to all of the people who worked so hard to bring this book into print at Madison Park Press, especially Christine Zika, Lisa Thornbloom, Jennifer Puglisi, and Christos Peterson.

—RKW

Thanks to my wife, Joanne Seminara, our children, Peter and Gabrielle, my in-laws, Joe and Anita Seminara, and the entire Seminara clan. And, of course, a great big thanks to Dr. Ruth.

—PAL

Introduction

*F*or more than twenty-five years I've been trying to help people have *terrrrific* sex. And while I may have been a pioneer in this movement, I certainly haven't been alone. Pay a visit to your local newsstand, glance at the covers of the magazines, and you'll see the word *sex* over and over again. The reason is that sex sells. And by the way, I admit that whenever I see that word on a cover, I buy the magazine. I wouldn't want to miss out on an article that might offer new information on the topic about which I'm supposed to be all-knowing, now would I?

All this information about sex in the media is a fabulous opportunity for you to learn all you can about this most basic and yet so intriguing aspect of being human. It's not just idle curiosity that should drive you to building your knowledge base about sex. A deeper understanding of your own sexual functioning, whether you are a male or female, will enable you to get the most from your sexual abilities. And now that it's so easy to get this information, you've been given the perfect opportunity to make any needed improvements. But there is one problem with the flood of information: it can lead to information overload, causing you to be more confused than enlightened. Sex shouldn't require a thick instruction manual. Basically, sex is a very simple operation, and couples shouldn't need to reach under their beds and drag out an encyclopedia each time the urge strikes them. That's why I wrote this book. I believe that by putting down some basic secrets of sex onto these pages, you'll have an easier time figuring out how to have the best sex ever.

Why You Need Help

The main reason you need any instruction at all in this natural activity is that although you don't have to know very much about sex if all you're trying to do is procreate, it's a whole other story if you're trying to get the most pleasure from sex. So while most people can figure out how to do "it," many need some advice when it comes to doing "IT!"

Another reason is that we're all unique individuals and so the way we get the most out of sex is slightly different for each one of us. So in order to engage in sex that maximizes pleasure, some guidelines are necessary. That's especially true if one or both partners have a special need of some sort, which is not all that uncommon.

The other big reason why every couple needs some instruction is that the two of you are going to change over time, and if you're not familiar with the approaching changes, instead of becoming just speed bumps, they can turn into hurdles or even barriers to having good sex. And you shouldn't fight change; you should embrace it. Boredom is one of the most serious challenges every couple faces, so change, even if forced by the passing of time, can help to push boredom aside, providing that you're prepared for the changes and head off in the right direction.

Following the secrets in this book is going to be relatively simple, but it will take some discipline. The easy road is rarely the best road. If you want to become an expert at any skill, from driving to cooking to participating in a sport, you need to learn the secrets and then practice them. And you have to admit there's nothing that beats a practice session in this area. But practice only makes perfect if the two of you are working together, following the same guidelines. Once you both have a good grasp of the secrets, you'll be free to improvise. In fact, I insist that you blaze your own trail because that's the only way that you'll keep finding the pleasure that terrific sex can bring.

As you know, I am always trying to get people to fight boredom in the bedroom. But to do that, you also have to accept change in every aspect of your life, because if your day-to-day existence together as a couple is boring, that will automatically lead to boring sex.

Because of that philosophy, I'm always open to new ideas, which is why when I was asked to write a book that would first be offered exclusively to book club members—rather than the other way around, which is what usually happens—I agreed. So I guess you could compare the birth of this book to a breech birth, where the feet come out before the head. But as the long as the baby is healthy, it doesn't matter, and it certainly shouldn't matter to you, the reader, as I put just as much effort into this book as I would have had it been published as a trade book first. But I always want to be honest with my readers, which is why I'm explaining to you the manner in which this book came into the world.

Dr. Ruth's
Top 10 Secrets
for Great Sex

Secret 1

Make Sex a Priority

I know there are people out there who say to themselves, "That Dr. Ruth, all she does is think about sex." Admittedly, I devote more of my mental energies than most people to the subject of sex, especially since I still maintain a private practice, which means I'm continually analyzing the sex lives of my clients. But I'm realistic and I don't expect everyone else to spend as much time as I do thinking and talking about this delightful subject, though sometimes I feel sorry for everyone else who has to think about data bases, sales charts, and everything else but sex!

You might think that with all the attention the media pays to sex these days, everyone's sex life would be full to the brim, but the truth is that too many of us allow our sex lives to be drowned under the flood of all the other activities fighting for our attention, from work and family matters to watching television, playing video games, answering e-mails, chatting online, or even doing something as old-fashioned as reading a book. And this, my friends, is a big mistake. Sex deserves a special place in all your lives, so whatever deluge of events is flooding your calendars, it's your duty to make sure your sex life has a safe harbor.

Many experts in human resources speak about a work/life balance, worrying that workers who spend too much time on the job end up damaging their family life, which then affects their work performance. My goal with this book is to convince you that, similarly, if your sex/life balance is way out of whack, you'll harm your entire relationship.

So why is it so important to give sex a special place in your lives? Obviously, sex is a source of pleasure and a way to relieve sexual tension, which, if allowed to build up, can lead to all sorts of psychological problems. But for anyone in a relationship, sex is also a key component of the glue that holds that relationship together. A relationship in which sex has been pushed off into a lonely corner is not a healthy one. It's an indication that something is amiss, that the couple's bonds are becoming more and more fragile, liable to permanent damage.

And by the way, this applies to couples of any age. Yes, younger couples may have sex more often, but sex deserves a place in every relationship, even if both partners are in their eighties or nineties, providing that health concerns don't prevent sex from being possible.

As an individual, you can't live without air, water, and food, but even I have to admit that you can survive without sex. (Not that I'm suggesting you should attempt a bout of celibacy, but you can.) But a romantic/sexual relationship, not a platonic friendship, does require sex to survive. We are all sexual beings. Whether we want them to or not, sexual urges arise in our brains on quite a regular schedule. You can try to shunt them aside, but eventually they'll bubble up into your consciousness. And even if you are distracted by a million things going on in your life, when these sexual yearnings arise in you, sooner or later they'll grab your attention. However, if your partner isn't in the mood, then what happens? In many cases, nothing, and if your sexual yearnings are completely out of synch, a sexual drought can go on for weeks, months, and even years. And the longer it goes on, the more damage to your overall relationship. So if you want to keep your relationship healthy, you, as a couple, must learn how to get your sex lives in synch.

Sexual tension need not be a negative force; if used properly, it can actually have quite positive effects on your relationship.

If you're having sex regularly, then the urge to satisfy this sexual tension is having a positive effect, as you're both fulfilling a need in the other, one that no one else in the world can do for either one of you (provided you're in a monogamous relationship, that is). However, if you're rarely having sex, or worse, never having sex, then the two of you have a predicament. For while good sex helps to bind a relationship, too much unrelieved sexual tension can do real damage, especially if one of the partners begins to look outside of the relationship for sexual satisfaction. (And that holds true whether this person is actually having sex outside the relationship or just contemplating the possibility.)

How Often to Have Sex

I'm often asked how often should a couple of this or that age be having sex. Statistics can't provide an answer to that question because it's really very individualistic. The two partners probably have different needs, but that's okay as long as they can work out how much sex is required to keep the relationship running smoothly. But I can tell you that if there's almost no sex taking place, then the relationship is out of balance, which will show up not only in the couple's sex life but in other aspects of their relationship as well. A couple dragging themselves through the sexual desert will find their relationship slowly drying up over time so that eventually it will shrivel up into a worthless state. So while I'm not suggesting that you have to imitate the proverbial pair of bunny rabbits, you do have to make certain that sexual activity remains a constant in your lives.

Spontaneous Sex

There's an idea, or should I say ideal, some people have lodged in their brain that says sex is always supposed to be spontaneous.

That can be a very dangerous attitude to adopt, and the following case illustrates this point:

CASE HISTORY *Jeff and Judy*

Jeff and Judy were in their midthirties. They both held full-time jobs and had two young children. To say their lives were full is an understatement. Jeff had to be on the phone with European clients early in the morning, so he would go to bed around nine o'clock most evenings because he had to be up at four the next morning. Since Judy had barely put the children to bed at that time, she needed to stay up to give herself some time to unwind, by either reading or watching TV. On weekends, the children loved to jump into their parents' bed first thing in the morning, which meant that Jeff, who got shortchanged on sleep during the week, often couldn't keep his eyes open on weekend nights much past ten. Because of this time schedule, slowly but surely their sex life had been dwindling, so that sexless week after sexless week would go by, sometimes adding up to an entire month. They both were upset about it, but when Jeff suggested to Judy that they set aside some time for sex, she rebuffed the idea. She felt that sex wasn't something that could be scheduled but had to occur in the heat of the moment, and she was of the opinion that if she no longer generated enough heat in Jeff, then something was wrong with their relationship. Clearly, that attitude didn't help their sex lives any, and that's when they came to see me.

Let me be very clear, I am all for spontaneous sex. But far more important than having spontaneous sex is having sex altogether.

*If two people can't get in synch spontaneously,
then they must schedule time and
circumstances for sex.*

It should be fairly obvious what a couple like Jeff and Judy should do with regard to scheduling time. Once a week they should both look at their calendars and pick a night when Jeff can either go in to the office a little later in the morning, or perhaps he won't mind having a little less sleep; and Judy should go to bed with Jeff at nine and they should make love. If she wants to get up afterward, she's free to do so.

There's nothing complicated about this method of ensuring that they have sex, but with couples in situations similar to Jeff and Judy's, if they don't plan to have sex, I guarantee it won't happen spontaneously. That's not to say their plans will always work out. If one of their children develops a stomachache that night, then their plans will go awry. But most of the time it should work. And then despite their different schedules, they can still maintain at least a minimal sex life.

There are, of course, other factors besides when you go to bed that can throw a monkey wrench into your love life. For example, with regard to this couple, allowing their children open access to their bedroom can be catastrophic. If they're going to remain a couple with an active sex life, they have to put an end to this habit of allowing the kids to get into their beds on weekend mornings. Friday or Saturday night would be a perfect time to have sex, but only if Jeff knows that he can sleep late the next day. To allow their children to decide when the parents are to get up on weekends is just not acceptable.

Another potential factor can be the location of where you have sex. If you're a couple like Jeff and Judy with young kids, just knowing they're sleeping, or supposed to be sleeping, in the next room can inhibit you, and stifle your sex life. Don't let that happen. Make sure that occasionally you can make love without having to worry about the children. For example, you could hire a babysitter on a Saturday night, leave the house at 6 PM, have dinner and then rent a motel room for a few hours. (Or go to the motel room first and then go to dinner, or bring a picnic dinner to the motel room, or any combination of the above!) Or you can ship your children to grandparents or other relatives overnight, or make a deal with friends who have kids and have sleepaways twice a month, with each set of parents getting a free night a month that way.

If finding the time and privacy to have sex is a problem at home, you need to make some changes so that your love life has a place in which to be nurtured.

In the case of Jeff and Judy, the children were contributing to the scheduling problems, but there are plenty of couples who don't have children living at home who also can't seem to find time for sex. For some couples it's a matter of the two of them working different shifts. Sometimes the reason is that a night owl is married to an early riser. For others a hobby or sport might get in the way, such as when a husband leaves for the golf course or the fishing boat on weekend mornings. In the end, it doesn't matter what the reason is for a sex life to have gone into hibernation; if scheduling sex is the way to get it going again, then that's what the couple has to do. And if part of the equation for setting the schedule requires some other changes, like a few hours at a motel, then such factors must be taken into account when figuring out the solution that works best for the two of you.

Vacations can be a good time to invigorate your sex life, but if you have children and share a hotel room, then that won't happen. My advice is to rent a house or condo with your own bedroom in whatever place you're visiting. It might seem more expensive, but the money you'll save on meals you can have at home instead of going to a restaurant will more than make up the difference.

Sex on a Timetable

When Jeff and Judy came to see me, Judy's immediate reaction to my suggestion about scheduling sex was, "I can't make myself become aroused. Sure I can lie there and let Jeff have his way with me, but I won't get anything out of it." Now with that attitude, you don't need to have studied psychosexual therapy to know that her prediction will come true and she won't enjoy it. But the fact is, Judy was wrong on two counts.

There's a French saying, *L'appetit vient en mangeant,* which roughly translates into "Your appetite will arrive on the next Metro once you've taken the first couple of bites of your boeuf bourguignon." It's a sensation I'm sure everyone has experienced: not thinking you were hungry when you sat down to eat but finishing every morsel once your taste buds were awakened by the first few forkfuls. (And if it didn't work, blame the chef.) The same principle can work with regard to sex.

If you climb into bed and allow your partner to work some magic on you with his or her fingers or tongue, I bet that you will become aroused. Of course you can force yourself not to be interested. If you concentrate on something unsexy, like the need to do your taxes, then whatever your partner does to you will be wasted.

But if you let your mind put aside everyday worries and focus on the sensations, assuming your relationship is a good one, then in all probability you'll become aroused.

If you have serious relationship problems, then no amount of physical ministrations is going to get you aroused, but in that case it's not just a lack of time that's keeping you apart physically, but a lack of desire to be intimate as well. If that's the case, then you may need professional counseling.

No One Should Be Left in the Lurch

I'm urging you to give scheduled sex your best shot, but I have to admit that there are going to be times when you just can't put aside the events of the day. The two of you are scheduled to have sex, but your boss made a snide remark as you were walking out the door that has you seething. If you're a woman, it may just not be possible to overcome those emotions and become sexually aroused. So you climb into bed naked with your husband, he does all he can to arouse you, and nothing happens. Do you merely say "Sorry dear" and turn over?

Whether you are a man or a woman, if your partner has become sexually aroused by this attempt to get you ready for sex, you have a duty to give your partner an orgasm.

Now this is easier for women to do, and it's also more likely that a man can overcome outside influences to become aroused, but whatever your sex, you still retain that duty. A man who can't get an erection can still give his female partner an orgasm using his fingers, his tongue, or his big toe. The problem here is circumstantial, not one of bad faith, and if you love your partner, you don't want to leave him or her frustrated.

A True Aphrodisiac

I don't believe in aphrodisiacs per se; for example, some people believe that eating chocolate or oysters can make you sexually aroused, while I say that eating anything can make you sexually aroused, providing you believe that it will. Scheduling, on the other hand, absolutely does have aphrodisiacal powers, more so for women, but it works for both sexes.

If in the morning the two of you agree that you'll be having sex that evening, and you allow yourself to think about the pleasurable moments that await you during the course of the day, actually stopping what you're doing and fantasizing about the night's activities, that will cause you to become aroused. Since women take longer to become fully aroused than men, such pauses for a little sexual daydreaming can be very effective later on. Even when you put aside those thoughts and go back to what you were doing (and please don't engage in one of these fantasies while you're driving), the arousal process will be continuing in your brain, subconsciously. Then, when you're finally in each other's arms, the arousal process, already warmed up during the course of the day, will start up a lot more quickly. So in this regard, scheduled sex has a major edge over spontaneous sex.

If you want to increase the arousing effect this anticipation can have, then use some physical reminders. For example, if a woman puts on some very sexy underwear in the morning, and makes sure that her husband sees it, it will leave an image in his head that will keep his engine purring all day; and every time she remembers what she's wearing, she too will feel a little tingly "down there."

Added Effects

By the way, when you're taking an active part in making sure that your sex life is healthy, I'm going to bet that the rest of your life takes on a rosier glow as well. If all you're doing is working, if your day is filled with nothing but chores, then that is going to wear you down psychologically. But if you know that the week is going to have some moments of intense pleasure, whether they're scheduled or not, then that will give you a lift. It's similar to the way that knowing there's a weekend coming up makes it easier to work through the other five days, or looking forward to a vacation makes the prior months more bearable.

You're Not Just Friends

Rest assured that an active sex life is also going to do wonders for your relationship. Sex certainly provides individual pleasure, but it also makes the two of you more intimate. Intimacy is very important in a romantic relationship. It's what distinguishes it from a friendship. However close your relationship with your best friend, the two of you are not intimate. You may share very intimate information with a best friend, but you don't kiss, stroke, fondle, caress, or give each other orgasms. Those intimate activities are reserved for one person in your life, your lover. Remove that intimacy and you become nothing more than good friends. But then that friendship becomes just one of many. It's no longer special. So to make sure that your relationship remains above all others, you have to maintain a healthy sex life together.

To maintain and increase your level of intimacy with your partner, make sure that you keep your sex life in good shape.

Don't Take Each Other for Granted

There are other ways of making sex a priority that don't involve a calendar. For example, if when you're home together you're always wearing your grungiest clothing, that's not sexy. I understand that after a hard day you want to get comfortable, but it's possible to dress comfortably and still remain a little sexy. I'm also not telling you that the only place you should shop is Victoria's Secret. But there's also nothing wrong with dressing up a bit in front of each other. Slobs aren't sexy, and if you always look like one in front of your lover, you're sending a message that you don't really care about sex. This also applies to what you wear to bed. If you cover yourself from head to toe in flannel, that may send the wrong message. In the dead of winter, it may be okay to cover your body in layers, but as soon as the temperatures start to warm up, leave some of those layers in your drawers.

Pay attention to how you appear in front of your partner.

By the way, just because one of you is dressed a bit more sexily, it doesn't mean that you're going to have sex that day or evening. The same is true if you hold each other, kiss passionately, or give each other back rubs. All these could lead to sex, but they don't have to. But such activities will increase the presence that sex has in your life together, and in the long run, they will also mean that you have more sex.

When I say not to take each other for granted, that also means in ways that may not appear to have anything to do with sex but are most certainly connected. For example, a father who changes diapers is actually being sexy. I don't mean to say that the act of changing a diaper is sexy, but showing enough con-cern for your partner that you don't leave her doing 100 per-cent of the child-care duties is showing that you care, and that is sexy. So included in the list of sexy activities are putting out the trash, doing the laundry, cleaning the dining room table, and filling the dishwasher. Anything that shows you care about your partner, even little gestures, is part of the overall program of making sex a priority.

Make a point of showing you care about your partner as often and in as many ways as possible.

The Role of Romance

Men don't necessarily require romance in order to engage in sex, but that's not true for women, at least for a good part of the time. Yes, there are women for whom a quickie is great, but even those women require some romance at other times.

Romance helps to free a woman, allowing her to make sex a priority. A romantic evening swaddles her in love so that she can put aside her worries and concentrate on becoming sexually aroused. Because men are not as affected by romance as women, many don't give it the importance it deserves. In other words, they dismiss it, or pretend to act romantically in a perfunctory manner that destroys the romance rather than enhances it. I discuss a lot more about romance in Chapter 6.

If sex is going to be a priority in a couple's life, then the man must accept the requirements of romance.

Be Realistic

This is an issue I'll be touching on in several chapters, but that's because it's important. Many people expect their love life to resemble what they see on television or in the movies. The problem with such expectations is that what you see on-screen, even on so-called reality shows, is only a distorted reflection of real life. Comparing yourself to characters you see is going to distort your view of your own love life. Just as you don't expect zombies to pop up every time you pass a graveyard or aliens to abduct you when you go to bed at night, don't believe that your love life is going to follow the script of the many pairs of lovers you've seen on stage and screen.

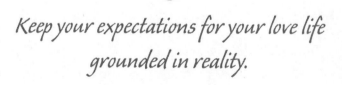

Keep your expectations for your love life grounded in reality.

Remember to make sure that your love life doesn't get overwhelmed by every other activity that's grabbing at every precious minute of your day and night. You must make it a high-priority item. Lovemaking doesn't have to take a lot of time, but it needs to happen with some regularity in order to keep your relationship healthy. So don't leave your love life to fall victim to the vagaries of chance, or you'll be gambling with your entire relationship. Instead, be proactive so that no matter how insane the rest of your life, having sex is part of the mix.

Secret 2

Know Thyself

For many people, sex begins as a solitary pleasure. Many teens have their first orgasm while masturbating. But soon enough the urge to become part of a couple and have sex with a partner takes over, and the focus of sex changes from a solitary one to a duet. (That's not to say that people who are in a relationship can't masturbate, but it shouldn't be the primary focus of their sex life. See Chapter 9 for more information about masturbation.)

In order to have the best possible sex, you have to understand your own sexual functioning.

In addition to providing pleasure and the release of sexual tension, masturbation is a good learning tool. But whether or not you ever masturbate, you do need to know the basics of your own sexual functioning, that is, how you react when engaging in sexual activity. This is important for both sexes but especially so for women. Many young women just starting out having sex with a partner have trouble achieving sexual satisfaction (and sometimes those early troubles continue later in life). And if a woman doesn't know what she requires to have an orgasm, she certainly can't expect her partner to guess. So if you run into any difficulties with getting sexual satisfaction from sex, or if you believe that your sexual engine isn't running on all cylinders, then the first place to look for the solution is not to your partner but at yourself.

List of Most Common Sex Problems

Men:
Premature ejaculation
Inability to ejaculate in one or more sexual situations, especially
    intercourse
Performance anxiety
Addiction to pornography
Psychological pressure caused by relationship
Psychological pressure from outside the relationship, for exam-
    ple, stress
Problems with sexual identity
Medical condition: alcoholism, diabetes, poor circulation,
    depression, and so forth
Side effect of medication
Not understanding changes that come with age, especially erec-
    tile dysfunction

Women:
Inability to orgasm (anorgasmia)
Painful intercourse
Psychological pressure caused by relationship
Psychological pressure caused from outside the relationship,
    for example, stress
Problems with sexual identity
Medical condition: alcoholism, diabetes, poor circulation,
    depression, and so forth

Side effect of medication

Not understanding changes that come with age, especially postmenopausal women

Separating the Sexes

In some cases, a sexual problem can stem from the same source
for both men and women, such as stress, but often the causes are
different. Some are very common, such as premature ejaculation
among men; while others are more rare, like painful sex among
women.

Some of the items I've listed are long term, while others may
come and go. What complicates matters is that if someone runs into
some sort of difficulty one time—for example, a man loses his erection during intercourse and then worries that there will be a repeat
performance the next time—those worries can cause the same failure to reoccur, irrespective of the original cause. And this reaction
can complicate the diagnostic process, because you might think
the problem you're facing is the original problem when, in fact, the
underlying cause is the fear that the original problem will reoccur.

If you are stuck in one of these vicious cycles, where worrying
that a sexual problem will reappear causes it to reappear, the
best defense is to concentrate on a very erotic fantasy to try to
block out those worries.

Sexual Myths

While some sexual problems stem from previous problems, others
are caused entirely by myths. For example, there are many women
who cannot have an orgasm from intercourse alone who feel that

they have a sexual problem. The fact is that a majority of women cannot have an orgasm just from intercourse. And an associated male myth causes some men to refrain from having sex because they feel their penis is too small to cause women to have orgasms, even though more than half of all women can't have an orgasm from intercourse no matter what the size of the man's penis.

Figuring out whether a problem you have is real or stems from sexual illiteracy can leave you confused. If you're suffering as the result of a belief in a sexual myth, the end result may be indistinguishable from a real problem. On the other hand, the cure is a lot easier than when the problem is more deep seated because in order to get out from under the woes caused by sexual myths, all you have to do is gain a better understanding of your sexual functioning. Once you can tell the difference between a real problem and one caused by a myth, you'll no longer be the victim of one of these sexual myths.

***

Make sure that you learn as much about your sexual functioning as possible so that you can avoid difficulties caused entirely by sexual illiteracy.

The Changing Myths

One reason that you might fall victim to sexual myths is that there are new ones that can snare you as you grow older. All men and women undergo physical changes as they age, and some of these affect sexual functioning. But if you are holding on to the mistaken notion that there's nothing that you can do about any of these changes, that they cause permanent damage to your sex life, then your sex life can get dragged down by the aging process. The truth is that you can adapt to these changes, assuming you don't fall victim to the myth that such changes spell the end of your sex life. For example, many women who go through menopause believe that this new stage in their life means their sex life is over, but that's not true at all. And as a man ages, he loses the ability to have a psychogenic erection, one that comes from his mind, not physical stimulation. He can still have all the erections he wants, he just needs some "foreplay." If he doesn't realize that, he might place the blame on no longer being attracted to his wife, which is one reason so many older men leave their first wife in favor of a younger second one. I go over these changes in more detail in Chapter 8, but I mention them here not because the changes themselves are myths, but rather because the hopelessness that can accompany them is such a myth.

The First Step

Whether you're the victim of a myth or have an actual sexual dysfunction, the first step in finding a solution is to recognize the problem. Back in Victorian times, a mother would tell her daughter on the night before the wedding, "Just lie back and think of England," meaning she wasn't supposed to get any enjoyment out of sex. That, too, is a myth because every woman can enjoy sex. However, if your attitude is that sex is never going to be enjoyable, then it becomes a self-fulfilling prophecy and you are never going to enjoy sex.

If you're getting far less satisfaction from your sex life than you believe is possible, rather than give up hope of making improvements, I want you to change your attitude and assume that you can make improvements. The first step is for you to examine your sex life to discover whether you're functioning at a reasonable level. I'm not saying that there isn't always room for improvement, but here I'm addressing those whose sex life is clearly not providing even a minimum of sexual satisfaction.

Those in Denial

One problem I often see in my private practice occurs in people who are in denial. Obviously, if you refuse to admit that you have a problem, then you'll never find a way to overcome it.

CASE HISTORY *Bill and Jean*

Bill was a premature ejaculator. He couldn't continue intercourse for more than a couple of minutes before having an orgasm. And once he'd had his orgasm, he was done with sex, which left his wife, Jean, completely unfulfilled. Jean had urged him to get help for his problem, but Bill refused to admit that he had a problem. So eventually Jean grew tired of having a sex partner who wouldn't take even the most rudimentary steps to satisfy her, and she ended up leaving him.

A lot of men won't admit to being unable to function in one arena or another, whether it be controlling their orgasms, repairing a faucet, or asking for directions, so they wind up making the same mistakes over and over. The important point is for a man to recognize that he has the problem rather than hide his head in the proverbial sand. Once he admits to having difficulties in this area, he can learn to overcome them.

Admit to your deficiencies so that you can begin to correct them.

Other Missteps

There's a long list of mistakes people make that have a negative impact on their sex lives.

CASE HISTORY *Ed and Fran*

Ed worked for a car dealer that sold American cars. At one point he'd made a good living, but as the American car buyers began to switch their loyalties to foreign cars, the sales at his dealership began to slip. Not only was Ed making fewer commissions, but he knew that there were too many salespeople on the floor, and since he was one of the oldest ones, he felt that there was a good chance he would be let go.

For several months Ed couldn't think of anything else but his job situation. He had been brought up to believe that the man should be the chief breadwinner, and he was too ashamed to share his worries with his wife, Fran. In addition, she had warned him a long time ago that he should get out of the car business and he hadn't listened, so that made him even more reticent to admit that he was facing the ax. Due to all his worries, his desire for sex plummeted. He tried to make love to Fran a couple of times, yet despite the initial erection, the moment he thought about his job situation, it would shrink. Because of that, he started to avoid having sex with Fran altogether. Since she didn't know the reason behind this sudden end to their sex life, she began to suspect he was having an affair. Their relationship started to deteriorate, and they found themselves snapping at each other for no apparent reason. They no longer showed any signs of affection toward each other, Ed because he didn't want it to lead to a sexual episode and the ensuing failure, and Fran because she was just plain angry at him.

The possibility of losing a job is one of those factors that can be enough to make a man lose his desire for sex, but it's certainly not the only one that can pry a couple apart for the wrong reasons. Here's another possible scenario: a wife works just as many hours as her husband, but she also has to take care of all the household chores. She resents this enormously but because she was raised in a household where her mother did all the housework, she doesn't speak up. So while her husband goes around oblivious to the fact that his wife is upset because he isn't pulling his share of the load, his wife keeps her resentment buried. As a result, she never feels like making love with him.

In both of these instances, the couple's sex life was in shambles, but with Ed and Fran, the cause wasn't the mechanics of how they were having sex, as it was with Bill and Jean, but factors outside their sex life. However, as in every sexual problem a couple may encounter, unless the two people involved can spot the source of the issues underlying their lack of sex, they'll never be able to make the necessary repairs to get their sex life started again. And far too often, when a couple's sex life breaks down completely, the relationship falls apart, and after a time, the entire marriage goes down the drain.

Now neither of these two situations, or most of the issues that affect couples, is incurable. But they can only be solved if both partners admit the problem and work together to find the solution. In other words, if you're willing to take off all your clothes in front of a partner and perform all sorts of intimate acts together, then you also have to admit your feelings, your desires, and your failures. And you can't do that until you admit them to yourself.

To fully enjoy sex with your partner, you have to admit your faults.

Being Honest with Yourself

In some instances, revealing some negative aspect of your sex life to your partner is going to be very hard, if not impossible, to do. But just because you can't face the thought of telling your partner doesn't mean you shouldn't recognize it yourself. Let's say a man isn't having sex with his wife because he can't keep himself from masturbating while he looks at porn on the Internet. While I don't think he has to tell his wife the reason he keeps turning her down, he absolutely must say to himself, "If I keep releasing all my sexual energy masturbating, my wife is going to get fed up with living in a sexless marriage and I'm going to lose her." At that point, his next thought should be "I've got to figure out a way to stop myself from masturbating so much."

Use discretion when discussing certain sexual matters with your partner.

I've asked you to be honest, and that's vital to a good sex life, but there is also such a thing as being too honest. There are memories, fantasies, and desires floating around inside your head that are better left where they are. There's a crazy idea out there that people need to find a soul mate and then completely bare their soul to that person. Whether or not there is such a thing as a soul mate, no one is immune from such human foibles as jealousy and prejudice. If you insist on telling your current partner everything you did in bed with past partners, for example, I can guarantee you that the reaction is not going to be entirely positive. And it may be so negative as to spoil the relationship entirely. The same goes for admitting to a sexual predilection that your partner may find revolting. So exercise some discretion when talking about sexual matters. If you're not 100 percent sure that a partner is going to accept what you are about to reveal, then leave that information inside your brain and off your tongue.

An Important Message

Let me say something important right here: you need to admit to yourself that you have a problem if it's seriously interfering with your relationship. One reason people aren't honest with themselves is that they haven't a clue what to do after they make such an acknowledgment. So they take what they presume to be the "easy" way out, which is to pretend that the problem isn't really a problem. The point I want to make here is that if you have a problem you can't cope with by yourself, there are ways of getting help. You don't have to tackle this problem alone. Many times the problem is beyond your ability to handle by yourself, so you must get professional help. You might need a sex therapist or a relationship or marital therapist. It all depends on the problem. Or it could be something like alcoholism or drug addiction, which will require a person trained to handle those issues.

If you have a problem that you feel you can't handle alone, seek out professional help rather than ignore it.

My Technique

By the way, what I do in my private practice is called behavioral therapy. I don't spend session after session trying to figure out if there is an event in a client's childhood that has triggered whatever problem was brought to my attention. I wasn't trained to do that and it doesn't suit my impatient personality. I want to see immediate results, which is why I prefer the behavioral methods in which I was trained. If you were to come to see me, my approach would be to give you homework, practical assignments, that will lead to changes in your behavior. This does not take very long. After a few sessions you should be making progress, so you shouldn't worry that going for therapy will necessitate a long-term commitment. It all depends on the type of therapy you choose.

And because not every insurance plan covers therapists like myself, some couples hesitate to get help because of the cost. In the short run that may be cost effective, but in the long run it probably will be just the opposite. If your relationship continues to go downhill, the end result could be a divorce. What that will cost you both in terms of money and misery is far worse than the cost of a few visits to a therapist.

Sexual Status Exam

When a couple comes to my office, I begin by giving each of them a sexual status exam. I always separate them, because people are not going to be completely honest in front of their partner (not that there's any guarantee that they'll be completely honest with me either, but the odds are better when it's a one-on-one conversation). Then I ask them very personal questions to determine the state of their sex lives. Now maybe you'll end up going to a sex therapist and undergoing this process, but for now I want you to conduct this exam on yourself.

Set aside some time when you can be alone and ask yourself about your sex life. You can write your answers down if you think that would be helpful, but you don't have to. All you need to have is a completely honest conversation with yourself about sex. This isn't a time for wishful thinking. I'm not asking you to fantasize what sex might be like with your favorite movie star. And while there's no way of avoiding the role your partner plays in all of this, your main focus has to be on your own performance when having sex. Eventually you might be asking your partner to make some changes, but the only changes that are completely under your control involve your own actions, or inactions.

Now I don't want you to think that you have to change everything you see as a potential negative in your sexual abilities. For example, if your partner has been asking you to perform oral sex and the thought absolutely disgusts you, then it's your right to turn her or him down. But on the other hand, if the only way your partner can have an orgasm is through oral sex, then you have to be willing to work with your partner to see what can be done. But again, before you can work out any compromises, you have to face the underlying problem.

No One Is Perfect

If you've spent half an hour thinking about your sexual abilities and you can't find a single thing wrong, then you're not trying hard enough. Nobody is perfect, and that's especially true when matching your skills against your partner's needs. I'm not only asking you to figure out whether you're satisfied with the way sex is done in your bedroom, but also whether your partner is.

And what if you don't know how your partner feels? If that's the case, then there's one strike against you right there. The two of you should be communicating about your love life at least at the level that allows you to understand whether he or she gets sexually satisfied as a result. It's true there are some women who fake orgasms, so there are men out there who honestly believe that everything is rosy when, in fact, their partner is not enjoying sex as much as she could, or maybe not at all. To some degree they could be forgiven, though most women are not such great actresses and I would bet that most men could tell if their partners are faking it.

Taking Baby Steps

I already gave you one reason why people gloss over their problems, and here's another that applies to people who have multiple problems: a concern that you would have to clear them up all at once. The fact is you won't be able to take more than a few baby steps at a time. People don't change very easily, and when it comes to physical changes, change may be impossible. (I certainly never figured out how to grow taller than four feet seven inches!) You have to be willing to change, yes, but how effective you're going to be at it, especially in the beginning, is another story. Effecting change, assuming it is possible at all, will take time, patience, and reasonable goals. In other words, it's a step-by-step process. Demanding drastic changes of yourself is far too threatening a proposition and is bound to lead to complete failure. But attempting to make one or two minor changes may be possible and will then give you the confidence to make even more. So don't be afraid to put down all your faults. In one sense, the longer the list, the easier it will be to choose one or two items to try to change. On the other hand, if you're faced with only one major problem, it could be harder to motivate yourself to fix it because you'll know that progress will be slow.

Accepting Blame

It's likely that when filling out your list, you're going to see some aspects of your sex life that represent your failures. That part of the list could be long or short, but there will be at least a few areas where you will realize that you are at fault. Now you don't have to include the entire laundry list when preparing what to present to your partner, but do include a few items. By admitting a fault, you'll affect your partner's attitude in a positive way. Remember, you're supposed to be lovers, both on the same team, not sparring partners. By making yourself a bit vulnerable, putting your defenses down, you'll be imitating what is supposed to take place when engaging in sex, because you're never more vulnerable than when you're having a powerful, all-consuming orgasm.

At that moment in time, the proverbial freight train could be crashing through your bedroom wall and you'd be incapable of dodging it. So demonstrating some vulnerability in this part of the process of improving your love life is a positive step. You're not trying to score points as individuals, you both get points when you both agree to make mutual adjustments to your sex life.

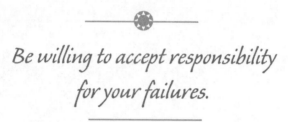

Be willing to accept responsibility
for your failures.

Not Limited to Sex

While you're scrutinizing your sexual behavior, you shouldn't limit your examination only to issues that obviously have to do with sex.

CASE HISTORY Mandy and David

David was an accountant. His job was tough but not physically taxing and since he needed a shower in the morning to become fully awake, his daily routine included a morning shower. But on some evenings, especially in the summer, he tended to smell a bit sweaty. This turned off his wife, Mandy. She wasn't silent about this, but he dismissed her criticism because it wasn't that he reeked of perspiration but that his underarms had a slightly pungent smell. The problem was that when making love, his underarms ended up being at the level of Mandy's nose, and so even though the smell wasn't very strong, it upset her. She started to avoid having sex, and he couldn't believe that it was over something as silly as a little smell. Eventually they wound up in my office.

The solution to this problem was quite simple. I told them that he could continue to take his showers in the morning, but before he went to bed he had to wash his underarms. He balked at first, but I got him to agree to try it for two weeks, and when he saw the improvement in his love life, it became a part of his nightly routine, like brushing his teeth.

Now while this couple could easily solve their problem, sometimes it's a bit more complicated. Men like, or even need, to see their partner's naked body in order to get aroused. But women who have issues of self-esteem may not permit this. No matter how often he tells her that he thinks she's sexy, she always remains covered up when he's around, and insists that the lights be turned off when they have sex. Certainly he's going to include this problem on his list of items to discuss, but this may be an issue that she is unable to deal with by herself. Issues of self-esteem can have very complicated histories that will require therapy to overcome. So does that mean there is nothing that a couple can do when faced with such an issue? Absolutely not.

She might have thought that getting help with her self-esteem problems wasn't worth the expense of going for therapy. But if she learns how important this is to him, then they might come to an agreement to budget a certain amount of money toward this goal. And even before they take that step, she might agree to have a low wattage bulb or some candle light burning, which will somewhat appease him. But they'll only arrive at these solutions if they talk about the underlying problem.

The Fear Factor

A limited budget may not be the only reason why you'd prefer not to have to deal with a certain weakness in your sexual performance. Another very common one is fear or, more specifically, fear of failure. What if you are a premature ejaculator and you now admit that it is a problem to yourself and to your partner. Now the onus is on you to correct this problem, but you're petrified that you won't be able to manage doing this.

When you were a child, what was the best way of dealing with that monster living in your closet or under your bed? Turning the light on so that you could see it didn't exist. The same applies to these fears you have about sex. And do you know what the light is? It's knowledge. Premature ejaculation is a learning disability, so while overcoming it can be difficult for some men, it's certainly not impossible. And there's a cure for just about every other problem having to do with sexual performance. You may have to exert some willpower, but you can overcome or at least manage the damage these problems are doing to your sex life. I still maintain my private practice and every week I help people overcome their sexual problems, so I know it can be done.

Getting Professional Help

If you weren't seeing as clearly as you once did, you'd go to an eye doctor, and if you had a toothache, you'd call your dentist. The point I'm making is that if you recognize that you have a sexual problem you can't handle, there is a professional who can help you.

If you need help from a professional concerning a sexual problem, get it.

There's a difference between what a sex therapist does and what an eye doctor or a dentist does. If your vision needs correction, you'll get a set of artificial lenses. A dentist may fill a cavity or put on a cap. In other words, your part in fixing the problem is a passive activity, at least once you get yourself into the chair. But when it comes to sexual functioning, I, as a sex therapist, would give you homework that over a short period of time would teach you new ways of having sex. It would be up to you to follow my directions so that you would be actively changing the way that you engage in sex with your partner.

While you couldn't sit by passively and hope to spruce up your sex life, as I said earlier, the homework I give is nothing like the homework doled out by your sixth-grade teacher. Given the negative feelings most people have for the term *homework*, I probably shouldn't call it that at all. (And sometimes I even instruct my clients not to do their assignment at home, but instead go to a nearby motel.) Nevertheless, to fix a sexual problem will require your active involvement. It's not enough to do a self-analysis, because you must then put some effort into fixing whatever you discover about your sex life that is in need of repair. This may be a little scary, but if you were to ask the people I've helped, they'd all tell you that it's definitely worth the effort.

One Never Knows, Does One?

This self-analysis should not be a onetime event. As the years go by, you'll change and so will your partner. In fact, you may even have a new partner, or two. (Hopefully, not if you're married.) So just as you go to your doctor for a yearly checkup, so should you do the same when it comes to your sex life. If you did a good job the first time, then each succeeding time should be easier. And spotting what needs to be fixed should also become more apparent. If your life has changed in many ways since the last time, you might have to make bigger adjustments.

Reassess your love life on a regular basis.

The dynamics of how you and a partner react to changing the way you have sex can be very fluid, and that's important to keep in mind. If your partner has seen you make some positive changes and stick to them, he or she might be willing to compromise more the next time you talk about it. If you've shown good faith, then your partner will be more likely to make changes in the future. If you're always ready to accept positive changes, you may find that your sex life ends up improving year after year.

Putting It All into Perspective

What's most important about this whole process of knowing yourself is being able to put it all into perspective. Whatever happens, don't panic. If your sex life is just average, you can make it better. And if it stinks, then there's even more room for improvement, so it's more likely you can make it better. But where this whole plan can backfire is if you put too much pressure on yourself.

This can definitely happen if you compare your life to what takes place in the movies or on television. What you see on-screen is life according to somebody's script, and that goes for most of the so-called reality shows too. And not only is there a script, but there are special effects and all sorts of other trickery to make what you see entertaining. So while I'm not telling you to stop watching, I do ask you to remember that your life can never compare to some director's fantasy.

And to some degree, this holds true for the lives of the stars of these features. With so many stars going into rehab, it should be obvious that celebrities shouldn't be emulated (unless you're talking about me, of course!). So many people think that because they emulate their favorite stars in some ways, like wearing similar clothes or perfumes, they can also safely copy their behavior. That's a misconception, because celebrities have so much more money that they can do things ordinary people shouldn't. For example, it might hurt celebrities financially to get divorced, but with their deep pockets, it doesn't really affect their lifestyle. But when ordinary people gravitate toward divorce instead of making a serious effort to fix their relationship, they might pay a price for the rest of their lives. Or celebrities can be single parents because the cost of child care is inconsequential to them, which is not the case for the average person.

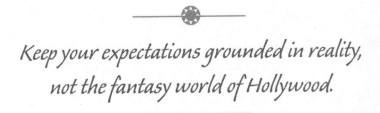

Keep your expectations grounded in reality, not the fantasy world of Hollywood.

Even Small Changes Add Up

If you prefer to live in a fantasy world instead of making small changes to your life, you're not going to be very happy. On the other hand, any incremental changes you make, though they may not seem like much, will begin to add up to something positive—similar to the way that money put into a savings account grows through the magic of compound interest. The interest starts to accumulate, and after a while the pennies grow into a sizable amount. The same is true of small positive changes you make in your relationship. If you're constantly making little improvements as the years go by, your overall relationship will get better and better. But if the only changes made are negative ones, then guess what the cumulative effect is going to be?

Getting Started

While not all of the secrets I'm going to give you must be followed in order, the secret about self-analysis is really the place to start. And don't waste any time either. As soon as you can, set aside some time to think about your sex life, and depending on what you discover, the next steps (including talking to your partner or making an appointment with a sex therapist) will become self-evident.

Secret 3

Know Your Partner

I'm going to assume that you've taken my advice on assessing yourself and now have at least some idea of your personal strengths and weaknesses with regard to sex. With any luck, your partner will have taken the same journey and knows his or her sexual status. Now the time has come to take the next step and develop a better understanding of each other's needs.

When you think about it, it's strange that two people have sex over and over again and still have such huge gaps in their knowledge of each other's sexual functioning. When you have sex, you have to strip down, and yet so many people manage to take off their clothes and at the same time wear a psychological shield of armor around themselves. Yes, sex is a private matter and most of us grew up in families that rarely if ever mentioned the word *sex,* which in turn developed an aversion in us to talking about it. (And, yes, even I, who talks about sex so much, still blush once in a while.) And yet once you begin actually engaging in sex, some of that reserve should disappear vis-à-vis your partner, or so one would think.

And it is changing, at least among younger people. Younger generations are more open and discuss their likes and dislikes frequently and in frank language. However, I still get plenty of questions from teens, along with people in the their twenties and thirties, which proves to me that not all young couples having sex are also communicating with each other, and that's even more true of older couples.

The Role of Fear

One reason for this hesitancy is fear. What are people afraid of? They're afraid that if they start talking about sex, they might have to become more open to changes in their own views of sex. Many people know what they would like to change about *their* sex life, but they're more wary of what changes their partner might ask for. And all it really takes is one particular aversion to something sexual to keep them silent. So if a woman knows that she would absolutely never permit her partner to have anal sex with her, and he's hinted that he might like to try it, she might adopt the attitude that it's better not to talk about any changes to their sex life than risk having anal sex put on the table.

This is a legitimate fear. If you start talking about sex, you can't know what your partner might bring up. On the other hand, if you never talk about sex, you also can't make any improvements to your sex life. You become mired in the status quo.

Taking Risks Like the Turtle

My favorite animal is the turtle. If a turtle stays in its shell, it's safe from predators. In order to get anywhere, it literally has to stick its neck out. And I want to encourage you to be like the turtle and take some risks in order to improve your sex life.

There are several ways you can handle your fears. One is to lay them on the table right at the start. "Look, honey, I know that we have to talk about our sex life, but I want to tell you right now that anal sex is just not in the cards, so don't get your hopes up."

There are some problems with this tactic. The first is that maybe your partner has no appetite for anal sex either and you received the wrong message. So you've made a point of drawing a line in the sand needlessly. By beginning the conversation with a negative tone, your partner may react in turn with a list of "nevers." When you start out in that manner, it's going to be more difficult to make the atmosphere positive.

The other problem is that saying "never" may actually be limiting yourself. I've used anal sex as an example, and I'll continue with it for now, but keep in mind that the list of taboos could be quite long, including everything from oral sex, the use of toys, the use of erotica, and so on. But what you have to realize is that there are women who find anal sex quite exciting, and some can even have orgasms from anal sex. If you try anal sex, you might find that you're in this group. And more important, if your partner tries something that you desired that he never wanted to do, he, too, might find it enjoyable.

I would never tell you to permanently integrate anything having to do with sex into your regular routine that you find distasteful. But you might consider trying a suggestion from your partner once, just to see how you react. You'll never know how you like something unless you try.

Some of you may fear that such a trial would be like opening Pandora's box, that once you agree to try something that you've always been quite negative about, your partner will never give up trying to get you to do it again. If you really believe that your partner's personality is like that, then maybe you have to keep some boxes closed. That's a personal decision based on your intimate knowledge of your sex partner. But that doesn't mean that you need to keep every box sealed tight. If you're going to make improvements to your sex life, you are going to have to introduce some changes, and they can't all be one-sided. Some compromise will be necessary.

Be open to new ideas.

Laying Ground Rules

Nobody ever said that a conversation about sex with your partner has to be a free-for-all. There's nothing wrong with laying some ground rules. In fact, the right ground rules may help you to make greater progress.

The worst outcome for a conversation about your sex life is a tit for tat. She says one thing, and he retorts by saying "And what about this, this, and that?" If this is going to be an argument, then the conversation should not take place. So perhaps you can make some progress by limiting the subject matter, and even baby steps would be a good way to begin, because no one said that this was going to be the one and only time you have such a conversation. To the contrary, they should occur regularly.

Topics

Whether or not you're going to limit the subject matter, what potential subjects might be covered in such a conversation? Here are some broad categories:

- Frequency
- Location
- Scheduling
- Erotica

- Initiating
- Pleasure
- Positions
- Distractions

Each of you should write down a laundry list of topics that you're interested in discussing. Then, together, decide which topics you're going to tackle first, along with the where, when, and for how long. Perhaps, to be fair, you could each choose a topic. I think that would be a good way of starting out. Don't choose the most difficult ones. Instead, open this process with a topic that you believe has the most potential for agreement. If you start off on the right track, when you get to the tougher questions, you'll do better than you would have if you had tried to deal with them right off the bat.

*Start the discussion about changes in your
sex life with something easy.*

Structure the Discussion

I'm not saying that you need a copy of Robert's Rules of Order next to you when you talk about your sex lives, but by having some structure, I believe the outcome will have a better chance of being a successful one. If this first discussion is too freewheeling, then you won't know where it could end up, and it could cross the line into uncomfortable issues. That would discourage you from ever doing this again, and that would be a pity.

The Gorilla in the Room

Having told you to keep the discussion simple at the beginning, I have to admit that that may not always be possible. Sometimes there is one major problem in your sex life that has to be addressed. For example, if the male suffers from premature ejaculation (PE) and because of it she's not having orgasms, then that's the number-one issue that has to be addressed. But there are several approaches that can be taken in this example, sort of like deciding which slope to choose when skiing, either the bunny trail, the triple black diamond, or something in between.

I'll stick to this particular example, PE, to explain what I mean, but obviously each case will be different, depending on the type of gorilla casting his shadow in your bedroom. I said that the male's PE was keeping the woman from having orgasms. Let's assume that she was able to have orgasms from intercourse with other men. (If she couldn't, then his PE would present a less worrisome problem.)

Naturally, she would want to have orgasms this way with her current partner but can't because he ejaculates too quickly. Now the ultimate solution to their difficulty is for him to learn how to control his ejaculations, but an interim step would be for him to give her orgasms in other ways (manually or orally) so that they both derived sexual satisfaction from having sex. Because of this interim step, a couple could be heading down the right road toward curing his PE, for there would be less pressure on him, which in turn would make it easier for him to accept that he needs to change as well as to effectuate that change.

What if after giving her orgasms outside of intercourse, he refused to take the next step and said, "Look, I'm giving you orgasms, so why do I need to control how long I wait to have mine"? That would be a problem, and perhaps one that would require the help of a therapist. If the reason he said this was that he was afraid that he might not be able to cure his PE, then a therapist could assure him that it was possible and help him achieve his goal.

What Else Can Go Wrong?

However well you plan for a talk about your sex life, there are no guarantees as to how it will turn out.

CASE HISTORY *Bill and Clare*

Clare was disappointed in the state of her sex life. She and her husband, Bill, had been married for three years and during the last year sex had become less and less frequent. She picked what she thought would be the right moment, a long car trip, to bring up the subject of their lack of activity in the bedroom. The end result turned out to be that Bill was thinking of leaving her for a man he'd recently met. It turned out that he'd had some homosexual experiences in the past and the lure of that lifestyle was just too strong for him to resist.

Obviously, this conversation did not turn out the way Clare had expected. But you know what? It was still better that he revealed his true sexual identity before he had done anything, because then he might have had sex with Clare again out of guilt, putting her at risk for a sexually transmitted disease.

If bad news is going to come out of your discussion, and especially if you have any indication that it might, don't let that stop you. You have only so many years on earth and if there's a serious problem in your relationship, the sooner you find out, the sooner you can begin the process of healing and going forward with your life. Hiding your head in the sand is not a good option. I'm of the opinion that you can't waste even a few seconds, so to spend weeks, months, or years in denial is just not something I can accept, and neither should you.

———————— ✦ ————————

Don't delay talking about your sex life because you might discover something very negative. The sooner you make such a discovery, the sooner you can begin making positive changes in your life.

But don't go expecting a catastrophe. In most cases, whatever problems a couple encounters are usually relatively mild. And the final outcome of any such discussions should yield a positive effect.

Keep Everything in Perspective

Now I don't want either of you to get your hopes up and believe that because of these discussions your fantasy sex life is about to come true. If you've been dreaming about having threesomes (which I don't recommend) or installing harnesses in the ceiling of your bedroom (which would be fine with me), the odds of either happening are pretty slight. To prevent disappointment, don't even think about such things. But perhaps if the two of you can make some subtle changes, a little down the line you might be able to integrate some changes that will satisfy some urges you've kept to yourself.

Begin conversations about your sex life with realistic expectations.

The Lost Art of Mind Reading

Just as I wrote earlier about how some people refuse to schedule sex because they believe only spontaneous sex shows real desire, a similar phenomenon occurs when someone doesn't want to talk to their partner about their sexual needs. Many people have the notion that their partner is supposed to somehow divine what is required. Look, just because you love someone doesn't mean that you turn into a mind reader. The most important sex organ is your brain, and while I know there are cows with built-in windows so that veterinary students can see inside, there are no such windows built into anyone's brain. The only way your partner can know what you're thinking is if you tell him or her. Telling a partner what you're thinking doesn't lower the value of this information, nor does it make changes that result in anything less worthy. The truth is that love doesn't make you clairvoyant.

That's not to say that you needn't attempt to read between the lines of what your partner tells you. If someone is shy, especially when it comes to talking about sexual matters, then that person may have difficulty saying what he or she is actually feeling and thinking. Your partner, or you, may not be able to get his or her exact feelings across, but there's a good chance that at least some clues might be dropped that someone who was paying attention could pick up on. For example, if a woman says something like "It would be nice if you spent more time on foreplay," that might mean that she's having difficulty having orgasms. Her partner could try to get some more information out of her, or simply spend more time on foreplay and see what happens. And when they are engaging in sex, her partner could ask if she's had enough foreplay before beginning intercourse. Because some people aren't very verbal, you can't expect everyone to be able to make the most of these conversations, especially when the subject matter is a delicate one like sex. But if you put some effort into listening, then you can increase their value.

You may not be able to read minds, but try to read between the lines.

Body Mapping

You may have sexual needs you can't talk about because you don't know about them. The advantage of being in a relationship is that the two of you can see if there's something more to learn by working together. In particular, I'm speaking of trying to discover what parts of your body are the most sensitive. If you've had many partners, and some were adventuresome, you might know exactly what feels best and what doesn't, but it's always possible that your past partners missed a spot, or that you've changed over the years.

In addition to having talks about your sexuality, I suggest that you also do some physical exploration.

Body mapping is not foreplay. It may turn out to be foreplay, but getting each other excited for sex is not the main purpose; that would only be an aftereffect. The goal of body mapping is for each to discover which parts of your bodies are the most sensitive to physical stimulation. For example, you might find bliss when having the back of your calf stroked, but if no one had ever done that to you, you might never know how good it feels.

There are a few rules for this exercise. Avoid the genitals. You already know that they're sensitive, and genital touching will cause you to rush, because the desire to have an orgasm will become too strong to resist. But other than the genitals, leave no area untouched. You might be skipping the lone spot that your partner didn't already know about. Don't limit yourself to touching. Licks and kisses create different sensations. The idea is to spend your time exploring. It's also important to remember what you discover. Sounds obvious, but because this exercise does usually lead to sex, some couples forget what triggered them into their eventual sexual frenzy. But again, let me remind you that actual body mapping is not foreplay, but a learning experience. If one partner discovers that a certain part of his partner's body is very sensitive, he or she is not to continue to stimulate it, but to note it and move on to see what other sensitive spots can be discovered. Later you can put the knowledge you've gained to good use.

The Sex Act

So now we've covered talking about your sex lives and physically exploring each other's bodies. Could there still be more for you to know? Of course, and what we've left out is actually having sex.

A number of years ago a book came out that first brought to light the so-called G-spot. Since I have always wanted to know everything about my field, I inquired of every gynecologist I knew if there was any such thing as a spot within the vagina that could lead to fabulous orgasms. Over the years I've probably asked hundreds of gynecologists this question (once in a while I attend medical conventions where I can boost my total), and not one could confirm that there was any scientific evidence for its existence. So my initial reaction to the G-spot was that it was a lot of nonsense.

But then I started getting lots of letters and e-mails from people telling me about their experiences with G-spot orgasms. That seemed to show that there was something to this, but what? Since I'm not a medical doctor, finding the cause of these orgasms was beyond the scope of my abilities, but what concerned me was the reaction of the public. While some people were reporting how much they liked this different type of orgasm, others were blaming their partner for not being able to locate their G-spot. So my position now with regard to the G-spot is that it's all right for a couple to look for it, but since there's no scientific proof that it exists, and the vast majority of women don't report having any G-spot orgasms, this exploration should be limited—and if no pot of gold is found, no one should feel bad.

I mention this because that's the philosophy I want you to adopt regarding sex in its entirety. There's nothing wrong with exploring your sexuality. Unless you bring other people into the mix (which I strongly caution against because it can wreck your relationship and open you up to the risk of disease), you really can't get hurt in this exploratory process. You might, as I mentioned earlier, discover something about your partner that you didn't know, something upsetting, but it was probably going to come to the fore anyway, so it's better to find out earlier than later. But if you adopt the right attitude, any exploring you do could pay off with some nice dividends.

How do you explore while having sex? First try to pay attention to what is happening while you're having sex. (I understand that when you do that, it might make it harder to have an orgasm.) It's called spectatoring. That's a word coined by William Masters and Virginia Johnson to describe a sexual dysfunction caused by self-focus rather than on the partner or one's own pleasure. Most people need to concentrate in order to have an orgasm and if you distract yourself by becoming an outside observer, it might prevent this from happening. But in this instance, it's all right to undergo this risk because you have a particular purpose in mind: the betterment of your sex life.

Oftentimes when I give my clients "homework," I expressly forbid them to have orgasms. It's not that I'm trying to be cruel, but in certain circumstances it removes excess pressure that can be helpful in solving a problem. I'm not telling you not to have orgasms, but only to make them your number-two priority. Your goal for this sexual session is to observe how you have sex. Certainly at some point you can stop observing and try to have an orgasm. I don't want to deny you. But I also must warn you that if you're too distracted, you might not be able to have one. But don't worry about it because this is not an exercise I'm going to tell you to have again and again but only this one time.

Under normal circumstances when you're trying to have an orgasm, communication can be limited because the very act of talking can make it too distracting to have that orgasm. But since orgasms are not the goal during this exercise, I want to encourage you to talk. Tell your partner what feels good. Ask for what you want; a little more of that, a little less of the other. If your partner is doing something wrong, you can even stop and make a point of demonstrating exactly what you would like. Use this opportunity to experiment. For example, take some pillows and place them beneath you in various ways. That will change the angle of entry of intercourse and you might find one combination that feels extra good.

Try Some New Positions

I'm going to be more specific about positions in a later chapter, but some positions can pose difficulties. They might not work the first time or you'll need some patience to figure out how to use them. A session like this, where orgasm isn't the goal, is the perfect time to try new things. If you're both trying to have an orgasm and you run into an obstacle, you might say to yourselves, to heck with this position, let's go back to a position we know. But in this case, you can give it a little extra effort.

If you have the whole house to yourselves, meaning there are no children about, then also make a point of trying out various places to have sex. Maybe having her perched on the kitchen counter would be a good place, even if he needs to stand on a phone book. And if you have kids, don't be ashamed to ship them out for an evening. In the end, you may decide that your bedroom, with the lock on the door, is still the best place for lovemaking. But if you find a special thrill in having sex on his weight bench, then figure out a way to lock the basement door from the inside so you can have a repeat performance. (Some people find that sex in the backseat of their car brings back fond memories and glorious orgasms. Just watch out that you don't get hurt, since you're not as young as you used to be!)

Baby Steps Are Good Too

Some couples have more complex problems that need to be handled more delicately. Let's say she thinks that she's too overweight and so she tries to hide her body from her partner. Well, if she's always insisted that they make love in the dark, then this experimental session may be limited to just playing around with some lighting effects. Or if he has problems with premature ejaculation, then you might want to work on the problem by actually using a stopwatch to limit the length of intercourse. (Curing him will take more than one session, but this could be a good way of getting started, especially because limiting orgasms is going to be a part of the learning curve needed to overcome this problem.)

Here are some things you might seek to learn during an experimental session:

- Whether or not she has a G-spot
- How to prolong his ability to control his ejaculations
- Positions that might be enjoyable
- Different places to have sex
- How to best communicate during sex, both orally and physically
- Household objects that might enhance sex
- Inhibitions you might overcome
- Learning to pace yourselves
- How to add romance
- Whether music enhances or is a distraction
- The role erotica might play
- The use of sex toys

Planning Ahead

As you get older, there are going to be changes in your sex life, no doubt about it. For example, most women, after they go through menopause, no longer produce enough natural lubrication for intercourse. The cure is simple: use an artificial lubricant. While it's not difficult to use a lubricant, it does change the atmosphere the first time you're using one out of necessity. Some people use lubricants long before menopause sets in for a variety of reasons. But here I'm suggesting that you try them out so that you become familiar with their use. Trying out various lubricants while you're in your forties will make it easier to integrate them into your love life later on when they become necessary. And who knows, you might find out that their use gives you enough enhancement right now that you'll want to make them part of your sex life even before you can't do without them.

On the male half of the equation, an older man will no longer have psychogenic erections, those that are caused by nonphysical stimuli, like a pretty girl in a bikini or an erotic thought. Once a man reaches that state, he needs physical stimulation to have an erection. And many men, especially as they get even a bit older, find that oral sex is the best or even the only way for them to obtain an erection. If a wife feels that she is being forced into having oral sex in her sixties, she may get upset. But if the couple have used oral sex before, even if only occasionally, then this change won't be as difficult.

The First, Not the Only

Since there are so many areas to cover, it's likely that you won't get to everything in one of these sessions. But if you both agree afterward that it was a worthwhile endeavor, then it certainly can be repeated. Just as your car needs a tune-up every so many miles, your sex life can also use a sprucing up every so often.

Put some time aside regularly to experiment so that your sex life can always be improving.

Orgasms

After you've been experimenting sexually for an hour or so, there's a good chance that one or both of you are going to want, or need, to have an orgasm. That's absolutely fine, but remember, this desire can't force a quick end to the experimental session. If one of you can't exert enough self-control, then I would suggest that you use a timer. Agree ahead of time that you'll be experimenting for, say, at least one hour, and that neither of you should have an orgasm before that. You might also decide ahead of time that intercourse will not take place, but that you'll use other methods to give each other orgasms. The advantage of that might be to take some pressure off the situation. There are numerous reasons why knowing that you were going to have intercourse at the end of this session could make it more difficult, and thus less valuable, so having such an agreement in place might be worthwhile. If you do agree to have more than one of these sessions, try it both ways, with intercourse afterward and without, and then decide which way helps you get the most from such a lesson.

Secret 4

Know the Kama Ruthra

Pardon the pun on the Kama Sutra, but let me assure you that there are more differences between this book and that ancient Indian classic than a play on words. Both books have instructions about assorted positions, but in my version you don't have to be a contortionist to try most of them. Even more important, because the brain is the main sex organ, my advice on how to have sex is tied in to how to use your brain while having sex, thus making it much more than a physical sex manual. I want you to be making love, of course, not just having sex. Nevertheless, variety is important to creating a vibrant sex life, so I strongly recommend that you try new positions.

Make use of new positions to stimulate
your brain and your heart.

Some Cautionary Words

Here's a point I made earlier, but it bears repeating at this juncture in the book. I certainly want you to have terrific sex, but I must begin with some cautionary words. If you think that because of reading this chapter, or any book that gives you different sexual positions, you're going to have the type of sex life you see in films, especially erotic videos, then you're setting yourself up for a big disappointment.

In erotic films the artificial ingredients include everything from orgasms to the desire to do whatever is happening in front of the cameras. The actors you're seeing are not performing sex acts for their own pleasure, but for the money. They don't have a relationship with each other and they're certainly not in love with each other. They're having wild sex, but they're missing out on most of the fun.

You and your partner, on the other hand, are going to enjoy the emotional aspects of having sex, but you probably won't get quite as wild as the actors in these films or in your ultimate fantasies. I want you to expand your sex life, yes, but I also know that if you have expectations that can't possibly be met, instead of enjoying whatever changes you make in your sex life, you might end up being disappointed.

In seeking variety, don't set yourself up for disappointment

Intimacy Is the Key

Two strangers can't really be intimate, no matter what they do together sexually, because while their bodies may be joined, they're emotionally and mentally disconnected. Intimacy comes from sharing yourself completely, and especially sharing your love for each other. Sex with someone you barely know is more like masturbation than intimate sex. Sex without intimacy can be pleasurable, I'm not denying that, but it's not complete. However, if two people feel as if they're one, then each experiences not only his or her own pleasure but that of the partner. Together they amplify the sensations that each experiences.

So establishing intimacy is a key to ensuring that other changes in your sex life have the most effect. Obviously, having sex in one position rather than another really doesn't add to your intimacy, for how much more physically intimate can you get than having a penis inside a vagina? But slowing down the action, so that you're not both rushing toward an orgasm, and are trying to feel every possible sensation that making love produces, is very intimate.

An Intimate Act

One aspect of sex that arouses some people is derived from the concept that sexual acts are somehow forbidden or "dirty." That is an immature way of enjoying sex and is incredibly limiting. The more intimate a couple is, the less guilt and shame they experience and what they are doing becomes less forbidden or "dirty."

Let me give you an illustration from another arena altogether to help me explain this point: drinking alcohol. Anyone can drink enough wine to get tipsy. You can drink the cheapest, most awful tasting wine and still get quite drunk. But when you drink the cheap stuff, maybe holding your nose so that you don't taste it as much, you certainly don't appreciate all the other qualities that wine has to offer. However, if you drink a fine wine, after having learned to appreciate its subtleties, while you may wind up feeling the effects of the alcohol, you'll also enjoy the taste, aroma, and the overall sensory experience that drinking fine wine entails. So the wine connoisseur enjoys his wine fully, even intimately. And he, or she, doesn't just gulp down the wine but, instead, swirls it in a glass to release its aroma, smells it, sips rather than gulps the wine in order to savor the many flavors before swallowing, and usually makes sure that any food that accompanies the wine complements it.

Having intimate sex is like drinking fine wine. You may have orgasms with or without intimacy, but you'll get a lot more out of a sexual liaison if intimacy is part of the experience. I can't say that immature sex is one-dimensional, but you'll experience many added dimensions when you have sex as an intimate couple. So that's why I want you to slow down sex so that you can appreciate all it has to offer and thus make it so much more intimate an experience.

Slow down the pace when you have sex to better enjoy the subtler pleasures.

The Sounds of Sex

How else can you achieve intimacy besides slowing down the experience? One way is a willingness to share your feelings. Clearly, you can pass on those feelings to a partner by allowing yourself to make noise when having sex. I say "allowing yourself" because some people have difficulty when it comes to making noise. In cases where someone can't focus enough to have an orgasm if they are verbalizing their emotions in any way, this is perfectly understandable. But most people who don't make any noise don't keep quiet because they're concentrating. Instead, they hold in these sounds because they're somehow ashamed of demonstrating how much they're enjoying themselves. So allowing yourself to express your pleasure out loud is an intimate act. And if you're truly making love and not just having sex, one way to make sure your partner understands how you're feeling inside is to say how much you love her or him.

Tell your partner how you're feeling by either using actual words or just making noises.

Giving Verbal Cues

In addition to giving voice to your emotions, I'd recommend that you also use your power of speech to give verbal cues. Obvious ones include such instructions as faster, slower, harder, or more gently. In other words, don't be afraid to tell your partner your needs to make a sexual experience the best possible. If using actual words is embarrassing, or spoils your concentration, then give physical signals. If a man wants some more physical stimulation to his penis, then all he has to do is take his partner's hand and place it where he wants it. Or if her hand is doing too good a job, so that he feels he might ejaculate too quickly, then he can gently remove it. Both lovers have to be attuned to their partner, recognizing that he or she is sending a signal that should be respected. And such moments are not the time to start an argument. If your partner is asking for a particular stroke, just do it. Later on you can ask why.

Let your partner know how to give you the most pleasure.

Baring It All

I can understand staying under the covers if the room is cold, but there are people whose desire to stay under the covers results from feelings of insecurity and low self-esteem, leading them to feel ashamed of their bodies. That shame cuts down on intimacy quite a lot. Visual cues are important in creating intimacy. For example, when a man sees that his partner's vaginal lips are all red and engorged, he knows that she is aroused, and he in turn becomes more aroused because of it. But if her vagina lies under the depth of several layers of dark covering, then that particular signal never gets exchanged.

This reluctance to bare one's body can derive from several sources. One could be from simple prudery. Some families are very prudish, and that carries over from generation to generation. But just as often the cause is one of low self-esteem. If a woman feels that her thighs are too fat, she may not want her partner to see her naked, even if she has no particular shame of her breasts or genitals. While I may have some difficulty convincing some of my readers who have this fear that their mates don't think as negatively about their thighs as they do, and may like them just the way they are, let me assure you that a male partner's desire to see your breasts and genitals will far overpower any negative thoughts about any other of your body parts.

It may be difficult for some people to get over their prudishness, and I say "people" because, of course, there are also men who don't want to be seen naked. The secret to overcoming such feelings is to take your time, because as I've said, if you're in a long-term relationship, as long as you're making progress toward positive changes, you'll feel the immediate effects.

One tip I can offer with regard to this problem is to control the lighting. You'll feel a lot less naked if instead of daylight or bright electric lights illuminating your every pore, you use candles so your body will be lit only by a soft glow. Installing a dimmer switch for your lights would have a similar effect, as would making sure one lamp in your bedroom has a low-wattage bulb that you use for just this purpose. And if you really want to take only a very tiny baby step, plug a nightlight into a socket, which will give off very little light.

Another way to strategically bare your body is to wear sexy lingerie. There are outfits that cover the parts of your body you're least fond of, but they bare other parts, or display outlines that your male partner will enjoy. Not only will this help your partner become aroused, but perhaps you can look at this as a step forward, so that after you get used to wearing such outfits, you'll be more willing to also go nude.

Finally, there's a place in the house that allows for nudity and coverage at the same time, and that's your bathtub. If you add plenty of bubble bath crystals to the bath water, you can be naked but covered by the bubbles at the same time. Invite your partner to share the bath with you, and perhaps turn off the lights and use candles. I'd also recommend a bottle of champagne because the effects of the alcohol might reduce your inhibitions somewhat.

Getting Too Intimate

Some people believe that in order to be completely intimate you not only have to bare your body, you should also tell your partner every last detail about your life, especially about your love life. I disagree with this view. If you tell a partner about past lovers, he or she is automatically going to make comparisons with them. That's not going to be helpful in creating your own, unique relationship. I'm not saying that you have to lie and claim you were a virgin before you met, but you can be honest while remaining vague. You don't want your partner to think that you're hiding something evil, but you don't have to reveal every little detail either. And I also believe in white lies. If you're a woman and your partner asks you how his penis compares to your previous partner, and in fact it's a lot smaller, don't tell him that. Why make him insecure? What does it gain you?

Of course, if you're going to keep your past shrouded, then you have to accept that you're not going to be able to probe your partner about his or her past bedmates. Just remember it's for your own good, because you, too, might feel bad after hearing about previous passionate affairs.

And definitely be very careful about revealing sexual fantasies. If it's one that is totally vanilla, like a trip together to a desert island, then you can safely tell all. But if it is at all kinky, you have to be certain that your partner isn't going to think less of you in some way, as the following case illustrates.

CASE HISTORY *Caroline and Andy*

Caroline had just finished reading a book about two housewives who ended up having an affair. While Caroline had never really felt any desire to have sex with a woman, the book had turned her on and she told her husband, Andy, about the feelings it had caused, just as a point of fact, not as a hint that she really wanted to have sex with a woman. But later that night when they had sex, Caroline seemed particularly turned on. Andy jumped to the conclusion that she was stimulated by woman-on-woman fantasy. He started thinking about it more and more. Then a few nights later at a restaurant he was certain Caroline was making eyes at a woman across the room. He asked her about it when they were driving home and she said that she had been admiring the woman's dress but nothing more. However, Andy didn't believe her and soon came to the conclusion that this was threatening their marriage. His solution? He went out and bought himself an entire woman's outfit and one night dressed up secretly and surprised his wife. He thought that he could fulfill his wife's desire to have sex with a woman by having sex with him dressed as one. Of course, since Caroline had no such desire, she jumped to the conclusion that all Andy's talk about her wanting to have sex with a woman was just an excuse to dress up as one and that he was secretly a cross-dresser.

This situation might seem comical, but when they came to see me, their marriage was in tatters. Andy's cross-dressing had actually traumatized Caroline and she wanted nothing to do with him. I was able to convince the two of them that this was all a mistake, but this example shows why you have to be careful when it comes to fantasies.

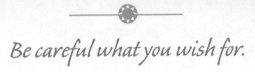

Be careful what you wish for.

Fetishes

Caroline had been shocked by Andy's "fetish" but there are people who have real fetishes. If, for example, you're a man who can't get an erection unless you're wearing women's underwear, this is something that anyone with whom you have a serious relationship is going to find out eventually. While you'll have to be careful how you reveal this, and make sure that the relationship is on solid ground, it's not something you can hide forever. But if you're a male who has fantasies about wearing women's underwear, but you can function normally without it, meaning you can have erections, then I'd advise you to keep this fantasy under wraps unless the perfect moment comes along. (For example, your partner puts a pair of her undies on you as a joke and you then let her know that you'd like to play this game more often.)

Let's Get Physical

Now you know how to set the mood with romance and what it takes to be intimate, so the moment has at last arrived to talk about actually expanding your sexual horizons. I'm guessing that you're not a couple of teenagers who've only had sex a few times. Instead, I'm going to assume that you've been together for a number of years and have had intercourse hundreds, if not thousands, of times.

That being the case, I could also assume you've mastered the missionary position, but sometimes assumptions can be dangerous, so I'm not going to do that. Instead, I'm going to assume that while you know the basics of how to have sex using this position, you're not as familiar with the potential pitfalls, some of which may be unique to the missionary position, although some are more general impediments to good sexual functioning that you could run into using any position.

The first one has to do with a woman's ability to have an orgasm. While it's true that some women can have orgasms while in the missionary position, many, the majority, in fact, cannot.

The key to a woman's orgasmic response is clitoral stimulation. For most women, having sex in the missionary position does not cause enough clitoral stimulation to trigger an orgasm. The sensations of a penis going in and out of her vagina are not sufficiently arousing because the penis doesn't come into direct contact with the clitoris.

Now some women, if their clitoris is sufficiently stimulated during foreplay, can become so aroused that they can have an orgasm in the missionary position just from the stimulation to her entire vaginal area that comes from the man's penis thrusting in and out. A woman may benefit from a pillow placed underneath her so that the angle of the penis's entry into her vagina is such that there is some direct penis/clitoris contact. The same effect may be had if the man "rides higher," that is, he moves up so that he maximizes the stimulation his penis and his entire groin area give her clitoris. (There are also gadgets that a man can wear on his penis that supposedly allow him to stimulate the clitoris, but somehow I doubt that most men could successfully aim for the clitoris wearing one of these.)

For those of you who aren't sure of what I just wrote, it's time for a quick geography lesson. The clitoris sits at the top of the vagina, under some folds of skin, above the entrance to the vagina, where the penis is inserted during intercourse. While intercourse causes some stimulation of the clitoris, it is not direct stimulation. If you make a circle of your thumb and index finger, and picture the clitoris as being on the knuckle of the index, and then push a finger from your other hand through the circle, you'll get the picture.

For many women, if the only clitoral stimulation provided during a session of having sex is that of intercourse, it will not be enough to cause an orgasm. So the missionary position is probably the one that is least likely to provide a woman with an orgasm, even though it's the one most commonly used.

Don't rely only on the missionary position to provide a woman with sexual satisfaction.

The missionary position may also pose a problem to some men who suffer from premature ejaculation. It's been reported that some men have the least amount of control over their orgasms in the missionary position.

Does all this mean you should never use the missionary position again? That would be going too far, but certainly if it's the only position you use, and the female half of your partnership never has an orgasm, then clearly your sexual repertoire is going to have to grow. The advantage that some other sexual positions have over the missionary is that they allow the man the use of his hands so that he can stimulate his partner's clitoris while they are engaged in intercourse. When the man is on top in the missionary position, he needs his hands to hold himself up. But when the woman is on top, then he can use his fingers to stroke her clitoris while she uses her body to move up and down the shaft of his penis. This combination can be effective in allowing some women to have an orgasm. The female superior also allows the woman to control the depth and speed of thrusting, both of which can be helpful in causing her to have an orgasm. And the man can also caress her breasts in this position, which for some women is critical in triggering the orgasmic response.

Some men don't appreciate not being in control when their partner is on top, but most adapt to this very easily. They want their partner to have an orgasm, and if her being in control is what allows this to happen, then they don't mind. In cases where the woman can only have an orgasm when she is on top, but both partners would also like to use other positions, all you have to do is separate your activities. You can use a variety of positions, knowing that at some point you'll have to use the female superior position so that she can have an orgasm. And, obviously, she will have to have her orgasm first because the man's penis has to be erect for her to climb on board. Younger men may be able to quickly have a second erection if they climax first while using another position, but as men age, the refractory period, the time it takes for them to be able to have another erection, lengthens; so for men out of their twenties, for the most part, having a second erection quickly enough to go straight to the female superior position after having an orgasm in another position becomes problematic. And if he starts to worry about whether or not he can have a second erection, then as we learned earlier, he's definitely going to have some difficulties.

A Caveat

Before I go on to other positions, I have to give you one more caveat, or warning. There are two components to an orgasm, the mental and the physical. Some women find that if they are actively engaged in doing something, like sitting on top of a man and going up and down, it is too distracting to have an orgasm. They need to concentrate only on the sensations to their clitoris in order to become sufficiently aroused to trigger the orgasmic response. So for such women it really doesn't matter what position the man uses; she needs to have her orgasm either before or after intercourse via direct clitoral stimulation.

Most of the women who fall into this category can get sufficient stimulation from either their partner's tongue or fingers to cause an orgasm. But some women need more than that; only the very strong sensations of a vibrator on their clitoris will do the trick. And some women can only do this themselves because they need a very exact series of sensations to cause an orgasm. In fact, there are some women who can only have an orgasm when they are using a vibrator by themselves.

I recognize that all of these scenarios are so far from the movies I mentioned earlier as to be disappointing. Couples want to give each other orgasms, preferably while the man's penis is inside his partner, and certainly without the use of any mechanical equipment. But since the main object of sex is for each partner to get sexual satisfaction, if using a vibrator turns out to be the only way for the woman to climax, then it's far better that she have orgasms in this way than remain sexually frustrated. Hopefully, her partner can use the vibrator on her, so at least he's sharing in the act, but if only she can use it, because she needs very specific sensations, then so be it. The couple can add variety to their sex life in other ways by utilizing a variety of positions before they get down to the business of providing each other with orgasms.

Be aware that if a woman had been able to have orgasms without a vibrator before she started using one, but then took up the practice during masturbation and got so used to it that she can't have an orgasm without one, then it may be possible to wean her off the use of vibrators. The way to do this is to have her use the vibrator to get close to orgasm, and then switch to human stimulation to actually trigger the orgasm, slowly shortening the amount of stimulation required by the vibrator. But if a woman has only been able to have orgasms with vibrators her entire life, I would advise against trying too hard to stop this practice because it probably won't work. As I said, it's far better for her to be able to have orgasms than to worry too much how she has them.

Position Options

For those women who can have orgasms from manual stimulation of their clitoris, using positions other than the missionary may facilitate having orgasms during intercourse. In addition to the female superior, another common position where this works is the side by side position, where the partners' legs are intertwined, like scissors. Here too the partners are facing each other so that the man can easily caress her breasts and face, as well as her genitals while having intercourse. (This position may also be good for pregnant women.)

In the doggie-style position, the man can reach around his partner to stimulate her clitoris and breasts. This takes a little more effort on his part, which may be distracting for him, but many couples enjoy making love this way, at least occasionally. This position can be achieved in several ways. If they're both on the bed, then they'll both be on their knees. But if the woman gets on her knees at the edge of the bed, the man can be standing. She could also be standing while bending over a chair. The trick with all these variations is adjusting for height requirements so that he is properly positioned to get his penis inside of her. If that's a problem, sometimes the use of a stool or phone book can help adjust any height variations that are causing difficulty. And remember, experimenting on how to fit your bodies together is part of the fun.

Using Furniture

Another type of position that allows the man to stimulate his partner's clitoris is when she is sitting on a piece of furniture, like a table, dresser or kitchen counter, facing outward, and he is standing in front of her. Of course, the piece of furniture must be of the correct height so that he can place his penis inside her vagina. Again, if you don't have a piece of furniture that matches your heights, the use of a stool or phone book may provide the solution. Most beds are too short for this position, but if you raise it up, and there are risers made to give you more under-the-bed storage that are well suited for this purpose, then she could actually lie down at the edge of the bed while he is standing, which could be very comfortable for both. This is a position that older couples should consider.

Chairs

An ordinary dining room chair also offers several options for having sex. With the man seated, the woman can straddle him, either facing forward or backward. The backward-facing option offers two advantages. First of all, she can keep her feet on the ground, which she probably won't be able to do when facing forward. (It will depend on her height.) This places less pressure on the man and makes it easier for her to thrust up and down. It's also actually more comfortable for the man to reach around her to get to her clitoris than try to squeeze his hand in between the two of them when she's facing him. My only caution about using chairs is that you not get too rambunctious—the chair might break under you and someone could get hurt.

By the way, there are chairs designed strictly for having sex. They include stirrups in which the woman can insert her feet, and the seat can be adjusted up and down so that the couple can set it to the perfect height. They're expensive, but I think one reason more couples don't have one is that they shout "Sex!" and in our society, even married couples are reluctant to admit to the world, or at least anyone entering their bedroom, that they have sex. You can also buy sets of foam pillows that allow you to adopt different positions comfortably. The advantage of these is that you can stick them in a closet when not in use, or just pretend that they're comfortable for watching TV.

Watch Your Back

For those who are more adventuresome, not to mention athletic, intercourse is possible with the man holding the woman up in the air while standing. However, this presents two problems. First of all, his hands are no longer free to caress her genitals. Second, it takes quite a bit of athletic ability and strength to hold this position for very long. And any man with a bad back shouldn't try it. This is a position you'll see in a porn film, but I doubt many people use it in real life. That's also the case of many of the positions offered in the Kama Sutra. If you want to attempt them, be my guest, but for the most part, the two of you would have to be pretty nimble to fit your bodies together the way the diagrams of that ancient text suggest, never mind make passionate love. There are other books, like *The Joy of Sex*, that have diagrams for many types of positions that are more adventuresome than the norm, but less so than what is in the Kama Sutra. I'm all for your trying some of them out, but while you're experimenting, don't get upset if you discover that most of them aren't right for the two of you.

Pacing Yourselves

After my last comment, this is a good place to bring up the subject of pacing. Often when a couple is having sex at bedtime, they may both be in the mood for an orgasm but they also may know the clock is ticking toward the next workday, which is coming far too soon. That's when you are more likely to have sex in bed using the tried-and-true means. But at other times, when you have more time, experiment a bit. And I would suggest that when you do this experimentation, you take your time.

The slower you go, the more aroused you should become, and the more aroused you are, the stronger your orgasm should be and the more pleasure you'll receive. So if the two of you are connected while sitting on a chair, for example, spend some time just being connected, without thrusting at all. Kiss each other. Stroke each other all over. Add as much love to the moment as you can. And also spend some time thrusting very slowly. You won't get an orgasm this way, I know, but it still will be very pleasurable as well as romantic, and that's the point: to turn sex into making love, not just having orgasms.

The Holy Grail of Sex

At this point, it's time to bring up the most sought after goal of intercourse, the simultaneous orgasm. If the two of you are going to feel the earth shake under your entwined bodies, then certainly you want to have it happen in unison. But while this is something commonly portrayed in movies, it's not so commonly found in bedrooms. The reason why it is difficult to achieve is because so many people have issues with how they climax that to find two people who have complete control over their orgasms in the same bed is somewhat rare.

Why is this so difficult to achieve? We have already discussed the fact that the majority of women cannot climax from intercourse alone. But now we have to examine the other side of the equation: the male's abilities, or inabilities.

Premature Ejaculation

There are many men who do not have full control of the timing of their ejaculation. The condition is called premature ejaculation (PE), and it's a learning disability, because any man can learn to gain the control he desires. But not every man afflicted with PE makes the effort, or even wants to. There are men who are so afraid that they won't be able to have an orgasm that they don't want to do anything to delay it. Or else they care so little about their partner, that they don't feel it's worth the effort.

Let me add something to the definition of PE. In many cases, it's obvious that a man has this problem when he either can't remain erect long enough to penetrate the woman or else ejaculates within seconds after doing so. But would you say that a man has PE if he can last thirty minutes? If his partner needs more than thirty minutes of intercourse to have her orgasm, and he can't control himself beyond thirty minutes, then yes, technically he suffers from PE. Certainly, many people, especially men, would say that if a man can last thirty minutes, he doesn't have a problem with PE. To some degree that's true, but the defining thing about PE is whether or not the man can continue intercourse for as long as he wants to. If his partner requires forty-five minutes and he'd like to be able to last that long and can't, then he has PE. On the other

hand, if a man's partner can never have an orgasm from intercourse alone, if she needs to use a vibrator or requires oral sex, and
he climaxes after a minute of intercourse, he really doesn't suffer
from PE. For a man in this situation, the optimum length of intercourse is up to him, not the two of them, because no matter how
long he lasted, she would never have an orgasm from intercourse.
So the bottom line with PE is, if a man would like to last longer, he
should know that it's not that hard to overcome PE and he should
get a book on the subject, or else consult with a sex therapist to
learn how.

---

*PE is not a physical disability but a learning
problem men can learn to overcome.*

Sorry that I took this detour from the subject of simultaneous orgasms and brought up PE, but it's a topic that needed to be
covered somewhere along the line, and it seemed the appropriate
moment. Let me now wrap up the issue of simultaneous orgasms.

Simultaneous orgasms in the missionary position are not for
everyone. But that doesn't mean that the two of you can't share
the added pleasure that comes from the synergy of shared orgasms.
All you might need to use is a different position. One way is to use
oral sex in the 69 position, head to toe. Any position that allows
the man to stimulate his partner's clitoris may do the trick, such as
the woman on top or the side to side. So if the two of you feel that
having shared orgasms is a goal you don't want to pass up, experiment in various ways to see if you can manage to do it, even if
only once in a while. Just don't get hung up on this goal. The most
important secret of good sex is that both partners have orgasms, so
it really doesn't matter if a couple can time them together or not.
In fact, the very act of getting the timing down pat can lessen their

overall pleasure, especially if they feel they've failed altogether because they didn't both get to orgasm together.

I'm not against any couple's trying to learn how to have simultaneous orgasms. And if they can do it easily and have them every single time, then I say bravo. But if this is proving impossible for you, don't feel disappointed. If one or both of you are having difficulties having orgasms at all, that's something that needs fixing, but if you think something is wrong with your sex life because you can't have them at the same time, I'm here to tell you to stop worrying about it.

Don't spoil the pleasure of having sex by putting too much emphasis on simultaneous orgasms.

Multiple Orgasms

Some women can have multiple orgasms. In other words they have one orgasm and then a few minutes later have another, or have a whole series of them. In such cases, if the woman is having these orgasms from intercourse, the man has to wait to have his orgasm until she is finished.

Multiple orgasms is another one of those sought after items. I'm here to tell you that to some extent multiple orgasms are not all that they're hyped up to be. Many women who have multiple orgasms don't have that one, very powerful orgasm that leaves them totally satisfied. They keep having orgasms that are pleasurable but don't fully satisfy them. Whether by having lots of small orgasms they receive more pleasure overall, I can't say, but it would seem to me that to have one very strong orgasm that leaves the woman completely sated is more desirable. Of course, there are women who have some smaller multiple orgasms before having that final big one that does the trick, just like in the X-rated movies. That's great for them, but everyone else shouldn't feel disappointed as long as they are having orgasms.

There are also some men who report that they can have multiple orgasms, though they only ejaculate once. This seems to require a lot of practice. Now any man who has the time should go right ahead and give it a go. But I'm afraid that most people reading this book have a problem finding time for sex altogether and don't plan on becoming sexual stars. But if it's a goal you seek, please go for it.

CASE HISTORY *Sarah and Gabe*

Sarah read an article in a woman's magazine on the G-spot, a spot inside a woman's vagina that when properly stimulated by her partner can trigger very intense orgasms; it may even be accompanied by the squirting of fluid. Sarah had vaguely heard of the G-spot before, but upon reading the article and learning exactly where it was, she decided that she deserved to have G-spot orgasms like everyone else. That night she told her husband that his job was to locate her G-spot and give her an orgasm. Gabe was quite willing to try, but no matter how hard he searched with his finger inside Sarah's vagina, she didn't feel a thing. They gave up that evening, but Sarah didn't give up on the idea. A couple of nights later, she had Gabe undergo a new exploration, and again he met with the same results. She berated him, and Gabe felt bad.

There were no more such experiments because Gabe started coming up with all sorts of reasons not to go to bed at the same time Sarah did. He started working till midnight or watching a game on TV that he just had to watch. Sarah, who was already mad at him for not finding her G-spot, came to the conclusion he was having an affair, and that's when the fighting really began.

The G-Spot

The search for a woman's G-spot contains the same trap as the goal of having simultaneous orgasms. People have heard of this G-spot and may come to the conclusion that if the woman is not having G-spot orgasms and sopping the sheets with liquid, something is wrong with their sex life. If a woman acts like Sarah and berates her partner, blaming him for her failure to embrace the rapture provided by a G-spot orgasm, it can lead to serious consequences, such as having the husband avoid sex altogether.

I recognize that some women report having such G-spot orgasms, but it's not an experience most women have. So to my way of thinking, we should rename the G-spot the ghost spot. Most people don't believe in ghosts, but anyone who believes they've seen one certainly does believe. So if a woman can have a G-spot orgasm, she should go right ahead and have them. And if women want to spend a limited amount of time determining whether or not they have a functioning G-spot, they should do so. But if their search seems futile, they shouldn't be disappointed.

One Model Doesn't Fit All

As you can see, there are many ways couples can have orgasms. As long as both partners are having orgasms, then all is fine. Some women, and some men too, have problems experiencing orgasms. This book isn't a total guide to sex, so I'm not going to cover every problem people may encounter. The only thing I will say is that if you're having difficulties you've been trying to solve for a long time, make an appointment to see a sex therapist.

Oral Sex

I mentioned position 69 earlier, which is when two people are head to foot and give each other simultaneous oral sex. There was a time not that long ago when any form of oral sex was considered daring.

But young people today have oral sex and don't even consider it to be sex, so it becomes part of the sexual repertoire they continue to practice as they get older. But some older people remain squeamish about the idea.

One of the reasons for this has to do with cleanliness. Since the genitals are also where urine is passed from the body, people who are hesitant to practice oral sex may be worried about the general issue of how clean the penis or vagina is. One way to get over this issue is to share a shower or bath together. If you've just cleaned your partner's genital area, then you can be sure of its cleanliness. And the act of mutual cleansing should be arousing in and of itself, and that may help you to overcome any reluctance.

Another reason some women won't perform oral sex is that they do not want their partners to ejaculate in their mouths. The way to get around that issue is to talk about it in advance and have the male vow not to allow this to occur, though of course there is nothing in the ejaculate that is harmful (assuming that neither partner has any sexually transmitted diseases, that is). Every once in a while I get asked the question about the caloric content. That is an absolutely ridiculous question. Whatever it is, it is so minimal that it should not be an issue.

But even if the man doesn't ejaculate in the woman's mouth, there's a good chance she's going to come into contact with another fluid that some people call precum. The Cowper's gland, which secretes a few drops of fluid before a man ejaculates, acts as a lubricant for when the ejaculate comes shooting down the urethra during orgasm. It's only a droplet, but it is a fluid and some women find it off-putting, probably thinking that it is ejaculate.

One method of birth control is called the withdrawal or pull-out method. This method involves the man removing his penis from the woman's vagina before he ejaculates. But before he ejaculates, he's going to release a drop or two of Cowper's fluid into her vagina. While the fluid that comes out of the Cowper's gland doesn't contain any sperm, there may be sperm remaining in the urethra from the last time the man ejaculated that can be picked up by the Cowper's fluid and then deposited into the vagina. While the odds of getting pregnant this way aren't high, they're not zero either, which is why the withdrawal method is not an effective form of birth control.

Of course, if the woman's only objection is getting liquid in her mouth, then the couple can consider using a condom. I understand that it's not exactly what he may have been fantasizing about, but he may agree to it on the theory that it's better than nothing. In addition, if his partner gets used to performing oral sex with a condom, she may later agree to do it on his bare penis. Remember that there are flavored condoms that might make it more appealing, at least to his partner.

I'm often asked by women who've never performed oral sex what they should do. My answer is to practice on an ice-cream cone. Take an ice-cream cone, pretend it's a penis and lick it, suck on it, nibble on it; just don't take a big bite from it! Then when you have the real thing in front of you, especially if you're getting cold feet, pretend it's that ice-cream cone. That should help you get over the first-time jitters.

Ever since the movie *Deep Throat* came out, many women feel that they have to swallow the man's entire penis, and since most women can't do that and start to gag very quickly, it makes them feel bad. As I've said many times, don't compare yourself to what you see in movies, porn movies in particular. Second, the most sensitive part of the penis is the frenum, the underside of the head of the penis, and you can do a much better job of stimulating the parts that give your man the most pleasure by not trying to swallow the entire shaft of the penis.

As far as cunnilingus is concerned, which is oral sex performed upon a woman, the man is definitely going to have to take some direction from his partner. That's because not every woman enjoys the same type of stimulation. Some women absolutely need their clitoris to get as much stimulation from the man's tongue as possible. Others find that when they're very aroused, their clitoris becomes too sensitive and they can't stand any direct stimulation. Those women need the area around the clitoris to be stimulated, which causes enough sensation for them to have an orgasm.

If you are performing oral sex on a woman whom you do not know is free of all STDs, I should add a word about safer cunnilingus. Some people use dental dams, which are pieces of latex, to cover the area. I really don't feel that these are going to be very effective—they're not really large enough. Because plastic wrap comes in bigger pieces, it can offer better coverage, but ordinary plastic wrap probably won't last and will rip. As I've said before, the best method for protecting yourself is to have sex only with one partner, one you know is disease free.

And how is the man to know what he should do? His partner has to tell him. She could do it verbally or else she could move his head slightly. If he already knows that there will come a point when he must stop licking her clitoris, that would be his signal. If he doesn't know this, then she has to tell him what is going on so that the next time he'll understand what he's supposed to be doing.

There are a couple of other issues that have to be addressed here. The first has to do with tired muscles. Some women take quite a long time to have their orgasm. What may start out as a pleasurable occupation for the man can soon get tiresome. No one's mouth and tongue are normally used in this way for very long, so after a while the man may actually be suffering a bit; but if his partner is moaning, "Don't stop, don't stop," then he knows he can't stop. One thing he can do is to switch from licking to sucking. Since your mouth uses different muscles for each, switching activities can serve as a rest for one set of muscles. And if your muscles or neck are about to give out, then quickly substitute your fingers. If your partner is very aroused, she probably won't care what part of your body is ministering to her clitoris as long as the sensations don't stop.

Anal Sex

Just as more young people are using oral sex to avoid intercourse, it's also true for anal sex. In order to remain "virgins," these young people will do anything short of having vaginal intercourse, and so anal sex is gaining in popularity. Some of this activity may be increasing because many more young people are experimenting with their sex lives than ever before and in this era of exploration (for example, having sex with people of both sexes), they'll try pretty much anything.

If two people enjoy having anal sex and they are doing it safely, then that's fine. If you're thinking about it as a way of expanding your sexual horizons, I have a few cautionary words. The biggest danger posed by anal sex arises when either partner has a sexually transmitted disease. Because the anus is not made for having sex, there is a greater chance of some tearing and bleeding to take place, which increases the odds of transmission of any disease. If both partners are 100 percent sure they are disease free, then this risk disappears; but arriving at that 100 percent without actual testing can be tricky because some STDs don't always exhibit symptoms. They can still be passed on and may have serious consequences in the next person to be infected. So the use of condoms is always a good idea. The use of lubricants is also a must, both to prevent injury but also pain. The anus does not provide any natural lubrication, as does the vagina, and so lubrication is necessary. There are some made especially for anal sex (Embrace) and they won't damage condoms, which will quickly deteriorate if exposed to lubricants you may already have in your medicine cabinet, like petroleum jelly or mineral oil.

As I stated earlier, there are women who not only enjoy anal sex but can have an orgasm from it. There are many more women, however, who never feel comfortable when having anal sex. This may happen as a result of both partners' inexperience. The ideal way of beginning anal sex is to first penetrate the anus with a finger or thin dildo. Once the person has become comfortable with the idea, then two fingers or a larger dildo can be tried. Eventually the man's penis can be inserted, though he should do so slowly and carefully. It's better to insert just a small portion of his penis at a time; that way the anus will accommodate itself more easily to being penetrated.

If a couple attempts anal sex with the man trying to quickly force his entire erect penis into the anus, as happens with vaginal intercourse, the result will probably be pain, and that will surely put an end to this experimentation. Of course, if the person being penetrated never feels comfortable, then they should give it up. No one should be forced into a sexual position that is not pleasurable.

Anytime the anus is involved in sexual play, and this includes stimulating the anus with a finger, both partners have to make certain that no fecal matter gets introduced into the vagina, because it is likely to cause an infection. It is important to wash either a finger or penis that had penetrated the anus before inserting it into the vagina. And if a condom was used, that condom should be disposed of. This may sound obvious, but you know what they say: s—t happens!

Other Orifices

When it comes to experimenting, some people will explore any possibility. I say that if you want to stick his penis in your ear or between your breasts, or if he wants to stimulate her clitoris with his big toe, then that's absolutely fine. I don't think that such types of sex are ever going to replace the more standard variations, but as long as you're having a good time, you have my approval.

No Pressure

Having said that, I am totally against anyone forcibly pressuring his or her partner into performing a sex act. No one wants bedroom activities to be boring, so to avoid that you must be a little daring from time to time, but there are enough possibilities that ruling some out shouldn't present a major obstacle. And remember, because you agree to try one particular position or sex act once does not commit you to doing it ever again. But while I continue to say that one partner shouldn't put pressure on the other, you might consider putting some pressure on yourself to expand your sexual horizons.

Not Everyone's Cup of Tea

I've just told you to try to expand your horizons, but there are some sexual acts that are just not everyone's cup of tea. Bondage, sadism and masochism, and some other sex practices fall into a category where I believe both parties have to share the urge or else these are roads that should not be trod. These practices can trigger very repugnant emotions, removing any possibility of sexual enjoyment. If both partners consent to trying out something a bit more unusual, that's fine. But if half of a couple is at all hesitant, then not only should that person have a right to say no, but it is the responsible thing to do because to acquiesce might end up damaging the relationship. So you have to exercise some common sense along with a sense of daring to find the right mix for you.

Arriving at a Game Plan

I've listed a few possible positions, but there are many others that no matter how much you want to use them, you'll find impossible. That's fine as long as you have the right attitude and approach these experiments with humor. It's okay to attempt to contort yourselves into a position that resembles something that would result from a game of Twister as long as you can giggle about it if it doesn't work out. Having the right attitude is the key to whether or not you've succeeded. If you're going to get all riled up because a position you're trying is not working for you, then it's not worth it. As long as you're both naked, fooling around with each other's body parts and enjoying yourself, it really doesn't matter whether or not you end up being able to insert part A into slot B in such a way that you can have something approximating intercourse. If it's not working, just stop and go back to having sex the way you normally do. How you wind up getting sexually satisfied is just not that important. So don't hesitate to try any position, but with the attitude that it's an experiment with no consequence if it fails.

Location, Location, Location

Using different positions is one way to spice up your sex life, but there are other ways as well, such as changing the location of where you have sex. Transporting your sex life into another part of the house has more to offer than merely a change of scenery. The furniture may present different options when deciding on a position. If you have a fireplace, making love in front of a burning blaze can be very romantic. The bathroom offers the added attraction of water, but don't forget that the bathroom can also be dangerous because of all the hard surfaces, so exercise caution. And speaking of hard surfaces, if you'd like to make love in a room that seems to be very sexy, such as a glass-enclosed breakfast room, but doesn't offer any place that's really comfortable, get an inflatable air mattress or even a yoga mat.

One of the advantages of beds is that the sheets are easily changed and cleaned if they get messy. Don't let that be an excuse for not making love on the couch, for example. Just place a nice absorbent towel underneath you.

Have you ever made love in a closet? Sounds weird, I know, but there's one thing a closet offers that you might not find anywhere else: complete, utter darkness. When you're in pitch black, close surroundings naked, you're going to feel vulnerable. You're going to want to be in each other's arms. You're going to feel closer. Even if you don't have sex, the experience will be romantic. Your sense of touch will feel heightened. You'll listen more closely to each other's breathing. Try it to see if it's not an experience that you end up finding intriguing, even if you never do it again.

What about making love out of doors? Having fresh breezes blowing over your naked bodies can be quite arousing, but you do have to take precautions against being seen, getting bitten, or maybe sunburned. One simple solution to these issues is to bring a tent. Some have sides that are mesh, so if you think you can safely leave the flaps up, you won't be totally visible if someone stumbles on you. You'll still be able to feel wind at your back while being protected from sunburn and bug bites. Inside a tent you'll be protected, but you'll also sense that you're in the great outdoors. Being able to have sex outdoors is one of the attractions of camping for some people, but you can experience it in your own backyard too.

And if the two of you ever made love in the backseat of a car, that might be someplace you could try again, just for old times' sake. Except that this time you might have your own garage, so you won't risk getting caught. (Don't run the engine in a closed garage, whatever you do.) But then again, maybe the risk of getting caught is part of the fun. Just keep those risks as low as possible.

Timing Is Everything

Many people have sex in bed right before they go to sleep. True, it's the most convenient time for many reasons, but if that's the only time you have sex, it could become boring. Parents will often wait until their children have gone to bed, but that's not an excuse to make love always at night. You could set your alarm so that you're up before the kids get up in the morning, or you might make use of a sitter and get away any time, morning, afternoon, or evening.

For older couples, having sex in the morning can be an advantage. Your body doesn't secrete hormones at the same rate throughout the day. Testosterone, the male sex hormone, is at its peak in a man's bloodstream in the morning. So if an older man has any difficulties with becoming aroused, having sex in the morning could provide the answer. Additionally, if you're both refreshed after a good night's sleep, then that also makes morning a good time for sex. If you're retired or on vacation, you don't have to make love as soon as your eyes pop open. You can get up and have your morning coffee, returning to bed a little later on, or even have sex right there in the kitchen!

***

Vary the time and places you have sex to keep boredom at bay.

Massage

I mentioned earlier that making love as slowly as possible is a good idea because it builds your anticipation and arousal. One way to delay having sex while doing something very sensual is to give each other massages. Putting oil on a partner's naked body and massaging it into his or her skin is a very sensuous act. Of course, massaging some parts of the body has a greater erotic effect than others, but that's what is good about massage: you can go back and forth between massaging erotic areas and those that are less so, delaying the time when you will actually have sex. And if you light the room with only candles, add some scent via some incense, and share a glass of wine, the experience can be as romantic as it is sensual.

Sex Toys

I don't particularly like the term *sex toys*, since I think of sex as an adult activity. But it's entered our vocabulary, so there's no point fighting this particular battle, because I'm certainly not against sex toys themselves. I do have a problem when it comes to those that create pain. I admit it's a personal problem, in that the idea of associating sex and pain is the opposite of arousing for me. I understand that there are people who enjoy such activity, but since this is my book, I'm not going to pursue the topic; it makes me uncomfortable.

On the other hand, tying someone up, not to inflict pain but simply to create a feeling of powerlessness, could be a situation that might increase both partners' pleasure, as long as you both take part in each role. And a light spanking on the behind would also inflict little pain but could potentially lead to a highly erotic situation. So as you see, I'm not against using some of the methods of the S and M crowd to a limited degree, but when it crosses a certain line, then I'm left with only a cold, empty feeling.

I do want to give you one warning about this entire area, however. One partner, who may or may not have had any predilection toward this sort of behavior prior to your trying it out, could suddenly find him or herself hooked on it. If the other partner had no desire to pursue this any further, this could start to pull their relationship apart. So while these limited sorts of activities involving bondage or spanking could be looked at as innocent, they could also lay mines in your path.

Of course, some "toys" are really only for fun, like edible underwear or washable body paints. A vibrator, which some people consider to be a sex toy, can also be categorized as a serious tool for a woman who absolutely requires one in order to have an orgasm. However, when a woman who can have orgasms with a partner uses a vibrator to aid in self-pleasuring herself, then it has a more playful quality to it.

By the way, in order to satisfy the rules of full disclosure, I must tell you that I have endorsed one brand of vibrator, except that it's not really a vibrator because it oscillates rather than vibrates. It's called the Eroscillator and while it's a bit more expensive than some vibrators, it's very effective.

Dildos

Some vibrators are penis shaped, but there are also penis-shaped objects called dildos that don't have any mechanical features to them. Some look identical to a penis, but others do not. While a dildo is something that you might think of as used when there isn't a penis around, that's not necessarily the case. Some women really crave the feeling of having their vagina filled, and if their partner's penis doesn't give them that feeling, then a dildo is a good substitute. A dildo can also be inserted into the vagina during oral sex. And then there are smaller dildos, also called butt plugs, that are used for anal play. You can even strap one into a harness so that a woman can wear it and have anal sex with her partner as if she possessed a penis.

There also exist penis extenders, rubber "overcoats" for a man's penis, that make it feel bigger to the woman during intercourse. All these devices can be easily and inconspicuously purchased online. Just search under the term *sex toys* and you'll find lots of Web sites.

Water Water Everywhere

Another method of providing stimulus to a woman's clitoris is by using water pressure. There have always been women who needed to masturbate but because of their upbringing, could not bring themselves to actually touch their vaginal area. By applying water pressure, they could create the sensations that were required to have orgasms. Back in the days when plumbing was more simple, women would lie down in their bathtubs, scoot their butts up against the wall of the tub so that the water flowing out of the faucet would fall right on their clitoris. Today there are all sorts of gadgets to spray water that most women prefer because they are a lot more comfortable to use and they produce more stimulation. And if you have a hot tub, then the jets from one of those will also do the trick. Of course, a spray of water can also arouse a man, though you have to be careful that it not be too strong, especially if it is directed at his testicles.

As I've mentioned earlier, much water play takes place inside the bathroom, which can be a good place for sex for people with self-esteem issues because psychologically it's a room associated with nudity. It's also a room used to impart cleanliness, and cleaning each other can not only be a sensual activity, but can also help some people overcome any limitations they have toward sex that stem from its being considered "dirty."

Sex Games

One category of sex toys are games that you play. You don't have to go out and buy a game if you don't want to. You can simply write down on scraps of paper various sexy activities, everything from kissing to having sex in a certain position. Put them in an old coffee can, and at a certain time each day or night, take turns reaching into it. It will add some spontaneity to your sex life and as long as you both agree to the limits of what is written on those notes, such a game won't present you with a need to push the envelope further than you might want. There are other ways to use such a "toy." For example, if you both took a vow not to swear, whenever one of you lets go of a curse word, he or she would have to reach into the can. (Hopefully, this wouldn't lead to the two of you swearing even more!)

But if you prefer to purchase a ready-made game, there are plenty on the market. Again, to disclose fully my part in all of this, there is a game with my name on it, Dr. Ruth's Game of Good Sex, though it came out so long ago that it might be hard to find. But if you can find it, I recommend it. You can find games in the privacy of your home by going to sites such as Eve's Garden or Adam & Eve. In fact, just looking around Web sites like these may provide you enough stimulation that you won't even have to make a purchase to become aroused.

Household Items

Just as water is something that is found in every home, so are lots of other objects you can use as sex toys, most of which will probably be located in your kitchen. There are certain fruits and vegetables that have a phallic appearance that can be inserted into a woman's vagina. For women who like the feeling of having their vaginas filled, and whose husband's penis doesn't quite do the trick, these can be handy substitutes. (Do make sure that they are washed first.) Smaller veggies could be inserted into the anus.

Other kitchen items that can make oral sex more interesting are sweet, spreadable products like whipped cream, chocolate sauce, or peanut butter. Both the act of spreading them on followed by licking them off can be quite enjoyable, even if a little high in calories.

If you happen not to have the proper ingredients for a night of food play in your cupboard, a shopping expedition could become an integral part of foreplay. If you both go to the supermarket and fill your basket with only what you intend to use that night for sex play, you'll find yourselves quite aroused in the process, particularly if you're only wearing sexy underwear under your topcoats. Be sure to examine closely the face of the checkout person to see whether or not they've guessed what you're up to by your choice of purchases.

Adding Partners

The orgy isn't a new concept; the Roman aristocracy used to have them with some regularity. Certainly, the idea of having sex with other people can be sexually arousing. I have nothing against using such fantasies inside your head, but when it comes to making them come true, that's where I draw the line. I'm sure you've heard of the myth of Pandora's box. A box was left in Pandora's care. Unable to resist the temptation, she opened the box and thus released all of the ills of the world, such as disease and crime. Once released, there was no getting them back in. Similarly, once you start down the road of adding extra people to your sex life, you have no way of knowing where you're going to end up. There are some people who get into swinging and their marriages survive, and for all I know, maybe even thrive. But there are also lots of other people who try this path and their relationships are completely derailed. The couple who wrote the book *The Open Marriage* didn't stay together, and I see couples in my office all the time whose marriages are in trouble because they weren't monogamous. In most cases, there's nothing I, or any therapist, can do about it. So while it's not 100 percent certain that your marriage will break up if you try the swinging lifestyle, the odds are high enough that I would strongly advise against it.

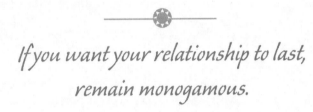

If you want your relationship to last, remain monogamous.

The Kama Nada

What if you have a partner who absolutely won't try anything new? What if your sex life is limited to a few positions, and on top of that, sex doesn't happen very often or at least not often enough for you? Is there nothing you can do to spice up your bedroom?

In my opinion, most of these types of sexual problems have their roots elsewhere. The main culprit is often a relationship issue. If one of you has negative feelings for the other, that's going to have a negative impact on your sex life. You should never allow relationship issues to fester, and if a lackluster sex life seems an indication that your relationship needs some work, then start working on it. In many cases, once the relationship has been healed, a couple's sex life gets back on track.

If it's not a relationship issue but one partner is having problems becoming aroused, then I would suggest that you try some minor adjustments to your sex life to see if you can't increase this person's interest. Why minor, you might ask? Because arousal can be delicate and if you try to jump-start a person's arousal with a major change, it usually won't work. But a minor adjustment might get this person at least heading in the right direction and with a little more patience, his or her sex drive may begin to get into a higher gear. For example, lighting your bedroom with candles on a night you're going to make love will add an element of romance. It's a sign that you care about more than just sex, and such a first step might free a partner with inhibitions to let go a bit more.

If the nature of your problem is frequency, I would suggest that you make dates to have sex. This will avoid unnecessary friction. What sometimes happens with couples that have differing sexual appetites is that sex becomes a combat sport. If he brings home flowers, she assumes that he's just trying to get her to have sex, and instead of reacting positively, she becomes angry, feeling pressured to have sex. But if a couple has agreed that the next time they're going to have sex is Friday night, and on Wednesday he takes her into his arms and covers her with kisses, this gesture will be loving, not sexual. His partner can relax and enjoy the attention because she won't feel under the pressure that this is only going to lead to a demand for sex. This kind of activity will act as a form of foreplay, working on her libido slowly.

There's a common mistake that some people make, which is to overreach. If a man's wife seems uninterested in sex, he'll bring home an erotic movie and ask her to watch it with him. Or if a man is not taking the initiative, a woman will walk around the house in sexy lingerie. In all probability, whatever put this person's libido into a slump is not going to evaporate because of added sexual stimulation. In fact, the opposite may happen. So if your sex life is barely treading water, take only small steps and also do whatever you can to find out the cause behind this lack of sexual desire. You'll be much more effective playing detective in order to get to the root of the problem than sexual provocateur trying to fix the problem by going over the top.

Secret 5

Kick Boredom
out of the Bedroom
by Kicking It out of Your Life

As anyone who's been in a relationship knows, emotional pairings can be quite fragile. One minute two people are madly in love and the next thing you know they've split up. Such a speedy ending is more likely to occur in relationships that are only weeks old, but there's no shortage of examples of relationships that have been around for decades that dissolve, though the appearance of a sudden end can be deceiving because the underlying cause may have been festering for years. The most obvious evidence of the fragility of so many relationships is that nearly 50 percent of all marriages end in divorce.

If you were on a mission to discover why this happens and you did most of your research by watching television shows and movies, it would appear that the main cause of all these breakups is the lure of some stranger seducing one-half of the couple. And because of this myth, many people become jealous when they see their partner talking to someone the least bit attractive. Now I'm not saying that this never happens, but I would guess that it is a rare occurrence in relationships where the bonds are strong. However, if the bonds are weak, then there doesn't even have to be another party for the relationship to fall apart. It might just explode, implode, or simply crumble quietly into a pile of dust.

So my advice to anyone looking under the bed every night to make sure that their partner isn't hiding a lover (figuratively speaking, of course) is to change focus. If there are any weaknesses in your relationship, they're unlikely to stem from external causes but rather internal ones. Now that's very good news, because if the weaknesses stem from causes within the relationship, that means that for the most part, they're under your control. But it also means that you must take responsibility for those weaknesses because strengthening the fragile aspects of your relationship will require planning and effort on your part. Given that the rewards are a rock solid relationship, these small duties shouldn't intimidate you.

Boredom

Relationships are complex entities with many factors playing a role in their overall health. For example, good manners are essential to a strong relationship. If one partner treats the other in a boorish manner, then there is little doubt that this behavior is going to weaken the bonds of their relationship. If one partner is a bully, then the victim may at one point decide that enough is enough. The list of all the factors that can negatively affect a relationship is a long one, but there is one that stands out, not only because it is important, but also because it is the one that is most ignored. That factor is boredom.

And I'm not talking about just sexual boredom. Two people can make love exactly the same way each and every time, without any variation at all, and still have a strong and vibrant relationship as long as they are experts at keeping boredom at bay in every other aspect of their relationship.

In fact, there are some people who get so used to making love in a particular way, sometimes a habit picked up during solo sex, that they absolutely can't have an orgasm unless they do "it" using a very rigid and structured technique. While I admit that that is not an ideal situation, as long as this person can have an orgasm from sexual encounters with his or her partner, it's not terrible either. Of course, such a person's partner is then stuck with following this routine, even though he or she might prefer at least a little more variety. But even in such special cases, if both partners find ways of adding variety to their overall relationship, they can survive such a scenario. Couples with a strong and vibrant relationship can survive most difficulties. Whatever the circumstances, love usually will conquer all.

But most couples are not locked into a rigid sexual routine, so adding variety to their sex life is both possible and desirable. However, if that's the only part of their relationship in which they make changes, in all likelihood that's not going to be enough to make their sex life or their relationship sufficiently healthy to withstand the many curves life may throw at them over the years. I would go one step further: I would say that unless both halves of a couple are open to change in other aspects of their life together, it is not very likely that they'll accept variety in their sex life. So dealing with boredom in your life in all its possible forms has two effects: it will strengthen your overall relationship and also improve your sex life.

Recognizing Boredom

Many people have a favorite TV show. Every week, on a particular night, they must be in front of the TV in order to get their fix of the favorite show. There is nothing wrong with this as long as it applies to one favorite show. But as that total grows, watching television could become more important than living life. And the closer a person comes to turning into a couch potato, the more boring they are as a partner. Even if a couple watches these shows together, the relationship is going to become stilted by this routine if it becomes a nightly preoccupation. I can promise you that it will have an impact not only on their sex life, but their overall partnership. And watching an excessive amount of television is only one of a long list of potential ruts that a couple can fall into, though it's certainly one of the most common.

Differentiating Ruts from Routines

If you have to be at work at the same time every day, you're probably going to set your alarm to go off at the same time on weekdays. That's not a rut, that's a routine that comes out of practicality. But if you have to have dinner at the same time every day, so the idea of going to the library before it closes or attending a meeting of your local political club or going to a summer lawn concert is impossible to schedule, then that's a rut. It's not imposed on you from the outside but is instead a hard and fast rule you've imposed on yourself, and it puts you and your partner in a box. And ruts are very boring.

No Visible Signs

When a person overeats day after day, it's easy to recognize the damage that is being done. All this person needs to do is step onto a scale. But there is no way to measure boredom. It can creep up on a relationship and slowly but surely suck all the energy from it until it is left lifeless. While this process is going on, the couple may have no idea how much damage is being done. There is no scale on which to judge whether boredom is affecting a relationship. So how do you avoid this trap? How do you keep yourself from being boring? The answer is simple; you have to make a daily effort to add vibrancy and meaning to your life.

I recognize that for many people this may seem to be a tall order. We all lead busy lives and some of you reading these words right now are saying, "I can't add one more thing to my plate. I can't go around every day trying to find a way not to be boring, especially if I'm not even sure that I am boring." I'm here to say, yes, you can.

Added Reward

Just as this book began with an examination of your sexual abilities, at this point let me ask you a related question: Are you bored with yourself? Do you wake up in the morning looking forward to the day, or do you dread it because it's going to be an exact repeat of the day before and the day before that? When you take honest stock of these questions, your life may not change drastically, but your outlook will because instead of settling for the same old, same old, you'll be actively looking for new ways to make your day, and yourself, more interesting.

Make your life more interesting.

How is this possible, you ask? Let me give you an example. Let's say that as a way to make yourselves less boring, you and your partner have decided to explore a new country in depth. For argument's sake, we'll pretend that the country you're exploring is Italy. How would this affect your workday? Since you're in your Italian period, you'll have stocked your cupboards with Italian foods, so if you bring your lunch, it's going to include some tasty Italian ingredients that are going to make you look forward to it more than usual. You'll have learned some Italian words or phrases, and during the day you'll be looking for ways to use them. So if a colleague at work stops by your desk to hand you a file, instead of saying "Thanks," you'll say "Grazi." And if you have any breaks during the day, you can pull out the index cards you brought with you and learn some new Italian words that you'll be able to try out on your partner when you get home that evening. There will be plenty of opportunities during the day to weave this new campaign into your daily activities to make yourself less bored, and less boring, during the workday. And best of all, you'll look at everything around you with that new twinkle in your eye—including that special someone in your life.

Better Sex Is the Reward

There is no magic pill you can take to become less boring. It's not like working on a tan, which only requires that you lie back and let the sun do the work. You have no choice but to devote some time and energy to this process. But just as there is a reward to sun worshipping, a glowing tan, there is also a wonderful reward to making your daily life less dull, and that's a glowing sex life.

For couples in whom boredom has set in, their sex life becomes more and more routine as time continues to drag on. When they were first together, they couldn't keep their hands off of each other, but then, as the months and years elapse, sex becomes less intense and less exciting. And remember, it's not just about using different positions. There are just so many positions you can use, so it has to be more than that. It has to be an overall attitude that turns sex into a more intense experience. And to enter that universe of heightened sexuality, you need to free yourself of the shackles of boredom in as many aspects of your life together as possible.

Your Most Important Sex Organ

The reason that a monotonous life spoils the joys of sex is that your brain is your most important sex organ, not your genitals. Tickling your partner's intellect has as much to do with foreplay as does tickling the fun parts. Reinvigorating your day-to-day life together will make the sparks fly.

I admit that sometimes I sound like a broken record, but there are certain points that must be repeated over and over again because so many people either haven't heard me or weren't paying close enough attention. And one of those points is that your most important sex organ is not below your waist, but on top of your neck, that is, your brain.

While it's true that orgasms result from stimulation of the genitals, they're actually registered and felt in the brain. And if a person has difficulty having an orgasm, and does not have any underlying physical problems, then difficulty in sensing orgasms lies not in the penis or vagina but in that person's brain. Let me give you an example.

CASE HISTORY Jerry and Eva

Jerry and Eva were in bed trying to have sex. Earlier in the day, Jerry's boss had chewed him out because of a mistake that hadn't really been Jerry's fault, and he'd spent the rest of the day stewing about it. While Jerry always found Eva very sexy, at that particular time all he could think about were the nasty comments his boss had made that were still echoing in his head. So while Eva did all she could to give Jerry an erection, he just couldn't manage to have one. Jerry knew why he was so distracted and did his best to explain it to Eva, but this had never happened to them before and so Eva was hurt, feeling that the real reason Jerry couldn't have an erection was that she wasn't sexy enough. That she'd put on a pound when she'd climbed onto the scale that morning hadn't helped matters.

The next time Jerry and Eva started to engage in sex, Jerry didn't have any outside issues to contend with. His boss had even apologized to him. But he couldn't help remembering the difficulty he'd had becoming erect the last time, and since he knew that Eva had been upset at his failure to have an erection, he was very anxious to make sure that the same thing didn't happen to him again. Because he was worried about being able to have an erection, however, this new worry had the same effect as what his boss had said to him and once again his penis remained limp no matter what Eva tried. This happened several more times, and because of this series of failures, Jerry felt more and more nervous before starting sex, almost guaranteeing that he wouldn't be able to have an erection.

If Jerry had tried to masturbate while looking at a picture of Eva without her clothes on, he would have had no difficulties making his penis erect. He didn't have a physical problem. His penis was in fine working order, but his brain was stopping him from getting aroused because it was being sidetracked by worry about his past failures. Jerry's situation isn't some isolated incident; it happens to many men. Not having an erection one time, especially if the cause of the failure is obvious, should not cause you concern. But many men can't stop themselves from worrying, and before you know it, that one time turns into a continuing series of erectile failures.

This particular problem has nothing to do with boredom. I'm using it to show you how important your brain is to the whole sexual panorama. If your brain isn't fully engaged in what you are doing, then there's a good chance your sex life is going to suffer.

Jerry's problem had to do with something worrisome. In general, those types of problems come and go. And, in fact, Jerry could have had a problem getting an erection that one night, but it might not have carried over to other times. Obviously, more serious issues, like actually losing a job or discovering that you have a life-threatening illness, can cause long-term erectile difficulties. But for most men, these are isolated incidents.

Boredom, on the other hand, has an entirely different way of affecting your sex life. Boredom won't have an immediate effect. It's not as if the boredom you felt toward each other earlier in the evening is going to prevent arousal later on in either partner. Boredom's negative effects are cumulative. It's when one boring day follows after another, slowly but surely turning into a boring life together, that problems arise, or should I say deflate, in a couple's sex life.

The reason behind this negative reaction to boredom is that the basis for sex appeal is not just physical but involves a number of factors. For example, your emotional reaction to your partner has a large role to play. If you're angry with your partner for some reason, you can easily understand why you wouldn't feel like making love with him or her. The same applies if your partner makes you feel disappointed, jealous, scared, disgusted, depressed, or triggers any other negative emotion. But if no such strong emotion appears to be affecting you, and though you still find your partner visually appealing but you're still not sexually attracted, the reason is probably boredom, even if you don't realize it.

Igniting the Spark

I know nothing about cars, but I do know that somewhere in the bowels of the engine are things called spark plugs. Their job is to ignite the fuel so that the engine can make the car go forward. You may have experienced having your spark plugs get damp on a very rainy day, which meant they wouldn't ignite and so your car wouldn't start. Boredom is like that damp weather that keeps your libido, your sex drive, from starting your sex engine. If life with your partner in general is boring, you're probably not going to want to engage in sex.

Notice I said if life in general was boring, not just your sex life. Now a boring sex life isn't a good thing. I strongly recommend variety in your sexual activities. But if your overall life together has some excitement to it, you can overcome sexual boredom relatively easily.

A Cumulative Effect

If you smell a wonderful meal being cooked, the next thing you know your taste buds wake up, as does your appetite. So in this case one sense, smell, turned on two others. Or if you hear a song with a lively beat, your foot may start tapping. Or watch a scary movie and you'll get goose bumps. So you see, our senses are all connected. That's why if you've spent an interesting day with your partner—which could be mentally stimulated by a visit to the museum, or physically stimulated by skiing, visually stimulated by admiring a sunset, or aurally stimulated by a concert—at the end of this day, you're likely to wind up having terrific sex.

In a long-term relationship, these events don't have to be directly connected. In other words, if over time you keep doing things together that are stimulating, in whatever fashion, then at the appropriate moments you'll become sexually aroused. But the converse is also true. If weeks go by and the two of you have done absolutely nothing that's interesting or exciting, then the desire for sex will remain at a very low level. And if when you do have sex, it, too, is boring, you shouldn't be surprised if your respective appetites for sex are going to grow dimmer and dimmer.

To have a good sex life, you have to make your life in general more interesting.

Solving the Problem

I'm not one to dwell on the past, so I want you to forget everything that made your life boring up until now. I could recite a list of issues and I'm sure you would pick out a handful that applied to you, but that's not going to get us anywhere. You want to move forward and that means you have to keep your sights on the future.

To begin, create a list of activities that you'd like to do that you're not doing. Some of these might be done with your partner, like going to the movies more often, while others, like going to exercise classes, might not.

"Hold it, Dr. Ruth," I hear some of you saying. "You mean if I go to exercise class by myself, I'm kicking boredom out of our relationship?" The answer is a qualified yes. Here's the qualification: your partner also has to make a list that includes doing something by himself or herself. In other words, if you're going out every night and your partner is sticking to his or her role as couch potato, then it's not really going to work. Or if one of you is going out and the other is staying home being resentful, that won't work either. But if he likes to bowl, for example, and she wants to join a book club, and they're both out on Wednesday night pursuing their own interests, then that's a positive step. When you both return, you should be invigorated, which should help you connect in many ways, including sexually.

I'm not saying that you should do everything apart, just that you can have your own pursuits, which can have a positive impact on your relationship. For this to be effective, it's important that your partner also has his or her own activities. Golf widows, for example, aren't profiting from their partner's activities. Sitting around watching the tube, whether it be football games or soap operas, also doesn't count. But since you're not Siamese twins (a politically incorrect term but it gets my meaning across), you can't be expected to share every interest and so you're both allowed to pursue stimulating activities on your own.

Of course, you also need to find activities you can do together. Start by making a list of things that would interest you. Get your partner to do the same, and then compare. Hopefully, there will be a couple of items that match. If so, you just have to get started. Don't waste any time beginning this process. You're trying to add energy to your relationship so you have to do it in an energetic fashion.

If you didn't find any matches, or if neither one of you seems to have any ideas of what you could do together (which is not a good sign, I might add), then let me offer you some general ideas that you can then adapt to your needs and circumstances. To make it easier for you, I'm going to group them.

Let's Get Physical

Doing physical activities together will result in good changes for your body. Physical activity releases endorphins, which make you feel better, so even a brisk walk together will be good for your relationship. And walking is one of those sports that allows the two of you to talk while you exercise, so this added time for communication will also have a positive effect on your relationship.

Unusual as it may sound, I also advise that you try kayaking, because it offers an opportunity to make you work as a team. If you're in a canoe or kayak, you have to synchronize your oars or you won't be able to steer. Acting as a team to accomplish a goal is an excellent way of helping to cement your relationship.

Winter sports are also very invigorating, since the cold weather can be quite bracing. I love to ski, but when I would go skiing with my late husband, we usually didn't go down the same slopes because he was a better skier. Just because you don't ski together doesn't mean your relationship doesn't benefit. Skiing involves taking a certain amount of risk. You should always be in control so as not to get hurt, but you also have to push yourself. There is a fear factor in skiing but once you've completed your run, you can't wait to hit the lifts in order to do it all over again. That's why if you've both spent some exhilarating hours shushing down the slopes, at the end of the day when you meet up back at the lodge for some hot chocolate or a hot toddy, you'll feel so alive that it can't help but give a boost to your relationship. It's this effect that makes me say that skiers make the best lovers.

Going to the gym together also counts, even though one of you may be using weight machines, while the other is doing aerobics. Again, you should both feel invigorated afterward, and you can talk about your workout, compare your results, and in the end you'll feel closer together.

There are also exercises that will bring you closer on two fronts. These are exercises you perform together. For example, if you sit on the floor opposite each other with the bottom of your feet touching, and then lean forward and lock your hands, by using a seesaw motion, each one holding the other as he or she goes backward and then pulling the other forward, you can get a good workout. And if you do an exercise like this in the nude, then it definitely will not be boring.

Another exercise that is similar to the one above has you standing back to back, locking your arms, and leaning forward and backward. As one partner leans forward, he or she will be pulling the other partner up into the air, which can be quite strenuous. (If either of you has a bad back, please don't try this. And you're also going to have to make adjustments for differences in height and strength.)

And wrestling, either in the nude or not, but more gently than roughly, can also get your heart rate going while being quite sexy too.

What about sports like golf or tennis? Absolutely, as long as you're doing it together. I have no problem with one of you playing a sport on your own, but if you use up a lot of your free time doing it, then you're not making repairs to your relationship. My goal isn't to get you into shape or have a great time, but to get you to reduce boredom between you. Obviously, if you spend too much time off on your own personal pastimes, leaving your partner alone, then that won't fulfill the goal.

A sport like tennis offers another benefit, teamwork. If you play doubles tennis, then you're both trying to beat your opponents, and learning how to do that can have a positive effect on your relationship. (If you're not into physical activity, playing bridge also allows you to work as a team.) However, you have to place your relationship above winning. If you start yelling at each other for making a mistake, then that's going to have a negative effect. So you have to judge your personalities before forming a team. If one of you is a lot more competitive than the other, then working as a team in a competitive arena may not be right for you.

Continuing Your Education

Taking classes certainly qualifies for helping to relieve boredom. Many colleges have continuing education programs where the classes offered are not part of a program where the students are trying to earn a degree. Larger universities may have literally hundreds of classes from which to choose. And other organizations, such as Y's and private companies like The Learning Annex, offer such courses as well. Consider taking a course that sparks both your interests so that you can do homework together and discuss what the instructor said. If taking classes ends up being something you both enjoy, and you discover different interests, then maybe one semester out of two you could split up.

Some of these classes may be more active than others. Classes that teach you a language or how to cook, paint, or sculpt require more than just absorbing information. Active classes such as these can give an added boost to reducing boredom because when it comes to helping each other, you will feel a degree of teamwork.

Broaden Your Horizons

One way of expanding your mind is to broaden your horizons. For example, let's say that the two of you like to listen to music but perhaps you've limited yourselves to one genre. Perhaps you both love country music, which is fine, but if that's all you listen to, it's intellectually limiting. I would recommend that you listen to some other types of music: classical, rock, opera, and music from foreign lands. For example, you might not understand a word of Portuguese, but the beat from Brazilian music is international and infectious. And don't just listen; do some research to inspire a better appreciation for these different types of music.

You could use the same approach to other activities. Don't just watch network TV; take a look at what the History Channel has to offer or your local PBS station. Instead of seeing the latest blockbuster, view a foreign film. And just because you've never tried food from, say, Afghanistan, if there's a restaurant nearby that offers a cuisine you've never tried, go for it.

Hobbies for Two

Sharing a hobby is another pastime that can bring you closer together and relieve boredom. It can be something that has a physical component, like gardening, or else you could work on a collection together. By the way, there's nothing wrong with working on two separate collections. Let's say you visit antique fairs and he is looking for old baseball cards and she is seeking out vases made of green glass. As long as you pay attention to each other, encourage each other, and share in the triumph of finding the perfect purchase, that's fine.

As you can see, I'm not suggesting that the two of you have to push this togetherness stuff too far. That could actually end up being boring. You just have to find ways of sharing your life beyond taking kids to soccer games.

And if I may be permitted to borrow from myself, allow me to suggest a short-term project that should pull the two of you together. In my book *Musically Speaking: A Life Through Song,* I describe the role that music has played in my life. At the end of the book, I suggest that my readers put together a CD of the music that has played an important role in each of their lives. This is a project that the two of you could do together. Your list could contain the music that was popular when you were dating, your wedding song, and any other music you find significant. This project will trigger many happy memories for the two of you, which will bring you closer together; then you can re-create those feelings every time you play the CD. And if you have children, you can make copies for them and explain to them the significance of the various tunes.

Use Your Library

Your local library is a huge resource for finding ways of fighting boredom. I would suggest that the two of you go regularly—if not weekly, then at least monthly. Either while you're at the library or ahead of time, decide on a topic that you'd like to explore together. It could be a historical era, like ancient Greece. Or gardening. Or the life of one of our presidents. Each of you could take out a different book on the subject you've chosen. Then as you each begin reading, you can compare notes. In other words, you don't have to finish your books to talk about the subject matter. And if after a few chapters you both decide that the choice wasn't the right one, then go back and try again.

Libraries offer not only a cheaper alternative to buying books, but they also add another dimension, a forced time line. When you borrow a book, you're supposed to return it after three or four weeks. That sort of deadline will help to get you reading. I know that you can usually go back and get an extension, but try to use the initial time frame as a way of scheduling this activity.

And finally, many libraries also offer the possibility of borrowing CDs and DVDs, so if you're hesitant about spending money to check out some music from far-off lands or an artsy DVD, maybe you can get this type of material from your library for free.

Volunteering

Another activity that can bring a couple closer is volunteering together. It could be for something purely benevolent, like a soup kitchen run by your house of worship, or it could be political in nature, like working on behalf of a candidate. Here you're helping people, but you're also helping your relationship. When you go home, you can talk about what you did, and how to do it better, and maybe what your next project is going to be. You'll also meet new people, which can also invigorate your relationship.

And if you get very involved in a particular charity, you might want to engage in a little fund-raising. For example, if you're working at a soup kitchen, you could ask your neighbors if they have any canned goods they could donate. Not only would you be adding to your time together by going door-to-door, but by introducing yourself to all your neighbors in this fashion, you might make new friends with whom to get together at other times, an additional way of shooing away boredom. See my next section to learn more about the benefits of making friends (though not friends with benefits!).

Friends

Friends can play an important role in making life less boring, though you have to keep in mind that they can have a negative as well as a positive effect. (The same is true for family members, but since you can't choose your family members, there's less that you can do about it.)

Instead of there being just the two of you trying to keep boredom at bay, your friends can lend a hand. And, in turn, you'll be doing the same for them, as boredom is a risk in every relationship, so by teaming up together, everyone gains. But for this to occur, you need some guidance. After all, four people can be just as bored together as two, and that goes for six and eight too.

A Word of Warning

The goal of this book is to make your relationship stronger. When it comes to friends, you have to be wary of those who tend to pull you further apart from your partner. If you have a friend who sucks up much of the time of one partner, then that person is driving a wedge between the two of you, and you know you're in dangerous waters when both of you allow this to happen. Let's say she has a best friend who comes over every night right after dinner, or calls, and they spend an hour or more talking while he goes off to watch a ball game on TV. Both partners may be happy with this arrangement—she gets to talk while he gets to watch the game— but this type of situation can be very damaging to their relationship. True, they're under the same roof, but they may as well be on the other side of town.

I'm not going to tell you that she should stop seeing this friend. What I would suggest in a situation like this is to be proactive. Husband and wife have to make plans ahead of time, and on those nights the friend has to be told that you're busy. And perhaps you even have to use some white lies. Let's say that your plans are only to sit down and discuss a book you're both reading. The friend may not understand your desire to do that, and so you may have to say that you have some important paperwork to do. Or if this person won't take a hint, then leave home and drive to a nearby bar or coffee shop and have your conversation over a cup of coffee or a glass of wine. The end result has to be that these nightly visits by the friend are no longer assumed by both parties to be nightly.

Making New Friends

For any number of reasons, the friends you've always had may not be the right ones for you at this particular time. I won't go into the whole list of reasons; after all, I'm not recommending that you drop them entirely, only that you recognize that you may need some new friends.

How do you go about broadening your list of friends? I would say just by keeping your eyes open. Maybe there are some neighbors down the block who look interesting. Or someone you always see at your house of worship but never socially. Ask a couple like this if they'd like to come over for cocktails, dinner, or dessert. If you hit it off, you've made some new friends. If not, then try again.

And if you're actively doing something, like volunteering in a political campaign or a soup kitchen, then you're bound to meet people with whom you share a common interest. That should be of help in making friendships.

Making Friendship Interesting

Whether it be with old friends or new ones, you have to make sure that when you get together you're not sitting around bored. If you have friends who are very lively and you never have a boring time together, then you may not need further plans. But if you have other friends who sometimes need a push to show some energy, then suggest some activities that will keep you all interested. You could bring out some games or make plans to go out dancing or bowling—anything that will make the evening offer all of you more than just dull conversation.

And if you have old friends you don't want to drop, but who, when you're together, just seem to suck all of the energy out of the room, then make sure to invite other people along when you see them. I understand that you'd feel bad about never seeing them again, but you only have so much time on this earth and you really don't want to waste too much of this limited resource on boring evenings you wish would end as soon as they begin. If you have other people who are more lively along for the ride, everyone will have a better time.

Armchair and Real Traveling

There's no doubt that if you broaden your horizons by traveling, you'll be kicking boredom out of your lives. But unless you're millionaires, you may not be able to afford either the time or money to travel continually. Perhaps you only have two weeks vacation a year and limited funds. Should that stop you? Not in my opinion.

Whether or not you are actually going to be making a trip, you can always plan for one. Experienced travelers never go anyplace without doing their homework. If you have limited time in a new city or country, you have to plan ahead to make sure you don't miss important sights, have so-so meals instead of gourmet ones, or sleepless nights instead of restful ones. But what if a trip to the Greek islands is not in the cards right now? Would it be a waste of time to plan for such a trip when you're going to spend your vacation at the same nearby beach you always go to? I say that it wouldn't be a waste of time to research a fantasy vacation because you'd be stimulating your minds whether or not you ever go there. By soaking up some Greek culture—reading some of the classic Greek literature, dining in Greek restaurants, and maybe even learning a few Greek words—you'll be broadening yourselves and your relationship will benefit. And these days, via the computer, you can really learn a lot about a foreign land. If you download Google Earth into your computer, you can zoom in on just about any spot on the planet to get a closer look, and Google Earth now posts pictures that people have taken via another Web site, Panoramio, so you can see even more. For example, if you want to see what the Acropolis in Athens looks like, there are probably a hundred pictures of it on Google Earth. If you do this for a few different places, you might discover that one of them will turn out to be a "must visit," and then you can work together to save enough money to actually go there one day. And, of course, having such a goal to work toward together will also help your relationship.

For those of you who would find it frustrating not to be able to visit a place you've been learning all about, then my suggestion is to pick a place in the past. It could be ancient Rome or Paris in the twenties or even your hometown at the turn of the century. Become experts in this time and place and you can turn it into an interesting hobby. Maybe you could find some old postcards to purchase on eBay (Paris in the twenties, not ancient Rome, of course, though you can certainly buy some old Roman coins). Or purchase prints from that time period to decorate your home. Or rent movies that have been set in your chosen era. By doing all of this, you'd be learning about this place without feeling frustrated that you couldn't actually visit.

And one more alternative is to become experts on the city where you live. Do you know its history more than vaguely? By spending some time in your local public library, and maybe seeing if there is a historical society that would also have records, you could learn a lot. And if you live in a town that was recently built, then just choose an older town that's within driving distance so you can explore it easily.

Here's one more suggestion: combine your interests. Let's say that while she likes the idea of traveling, he's not thrilled with it. He loves baseball. In that case, this couple could plan trips around baseball. They could pick times and cities where his favorite teams are playing. This way she would satisfy her desire to travel while he could boast of having visited some of the nation's famous ballparks.

If you use some creativity, you can come up with lots of ways to pair activities so that each half of the couple will get sufficient enjoyment out of it and will find spending time on the other's pastime worthwhile.

Games, Puzzles, and the Like

There's a huge world of games and puzzles to explore. As long as you do this together, it will bring you closer. Remember, part of the effect of boredom is that you may live together but don't interact very much, or only on a superficial level. If you play a game together, whether it be something intellectually challenging, like chess (and neither one of you has to be good at it); or based on chance, like Monopoly; or even silly, like Twister, such games will provide ways of bringing you closer together. You may not be able to base a relationship on playing Parcheesi, but you have to start somewhere and if that's the first step, then go ahead and take it.

Word puzzles, like crosswords, give you an opportunity to work as a team, competing against the puzzle rather than against each other, which is good. I want you to get out of your rut, and that's going to take teamwork, so anything that gets you in the right frame of mind is appropriate. And using your mind in this manner is also a form of exercise, which some people believe can help you lower your risk of Alzheimer's or dementia.

And, of course, when it comes to games of chance, like card games, you can always incorporate some sexual play into them. Even if you've seen each other naked a thousand times, playing strip poker will still have an erotic effect. But it doesn't have to be poker, a game in which the stripping will go quickly if one person loses several hands in a row! You could adapt the rules of any game, even a game like Monopoly, which can take hours to play, to add an element of stripping in order to add that erotic fillip.

Role-Playing

As two people go through life together, they end up taking on certain roles. Stereotypically she cooks and he mows the lawn, for example. Those are the obvious roles, but there are many others you've each donned that you may not even notice. Because these roles lock you into doing things the same way all the time, one way of breaking such routines is to take on other roles. There are many ways of doing this, some of which are simple and others more elaborate.

An example of a simple one is to literally reverse your roles at home, so that for a period of time, which could be one day to one month, he does all the cooking and she does all the mowing. Or else, in this scenario, you could share roles, so that he would help with the cooking and she would help with the lawn care, and do these things together.

But you can also change roles for a time by playacting. She could be Cleopatra and he could be Marc Antony. Or Napoleon and Josephine. Or even Homer and Marge Simpson. You could dress up or not. If the roles you choose are from a movie, you could rent the film or get a script, and even memorize some parts and literally act them out. Then, after having gotten in the mood, you could improvise so that you could continue in the roles.

Such role-playing is challenging, I admit. And a bit daring too. But it will certainly get you out of your rut. And the point isn't to be great actors, but to have fun together, and it should be just that: fun. If you find that you both really enjoy role-playing and have some talent for it, then maybe you could join a local acting group and take this up as a shared hobby.

Another type of role-playing you could try is to pretend that you're strangers who meet in a bar. Yes, you'll feel a little silly, because after all you're not strangers, but if you allow yourself to get into doing such a scene, after the initial awkwardness you should be able to get into it and perhaps you'll find it entertaining and maybe even educational. You might even learn something about each other. And you won't be bored.

For this to succeed, you have to decide ahead of time, to yourself, who you are. Remember, you're not you waiting in that bar for your spouse, it's the character you've chosen waiting to meet some stranger. If you've always wanted to be a model, then when the "stranger" sits down next to you and asks what you do, you say that you're a model. If he wants to pretend he's a rock star, then that's who he'll be. This allows for endless possibilities and makes it more interesting. When you first "meet," you won't know ahead of time who it is you're meeting. If it turns out that you each like a particular character, you can repeat the scenario, but I would recommend adding as much variety as possible.

And speaking of variety, if you then wind up in bed, make sure not to make love the way you normally do; after all, you're different people. This might even allow you to try positions you wouldn't normally try, since it wouldn't be you having sex but the character you've chosen to be for the evening. Then if you didn't like that position, as long as you didn't take on that role again, you could tell your partner that you don't want to ever employ it again.

Can anything permanent come out of such role-playing? It most definitely can. Let's go back to the above example. You pretended to be a model because it was something you'd always wanted to do: prance about in front of a camera trying on different looks. When you talk about the evening at some later point, and when your partner asks you why you chose that particular role, let him know of this desire. Then maybe you can actually make this fantasy happen, with your partner acting as the photographer. If you both enjoy the experience, then you won't feel guilty buying the latest fashions because you both know it will be part of this fantasy. And as you both get better at it, you can develop a portfolio of photos, not to show anyone in the modeling business, but as a combined hobby that can bring you both a lot of enjoyment. You could even set up a studio in your basement with lights and a backdrop.

Is living out such a fantasy silly? I suppose the answer is yes, but there's nothing wrong with being silly; there are enough opportunities in life to be serious, that's for certain. But by sharing this hobby, silly or not, you'll be pushing boredom away. You'll have fun not only during the photo shoots, but planning for them.

And if your partner had played a rock star, then maybe you could buy a karaoke machine and together sing songs, letting him play out his fantasy. It doesn't matter what the fantasy is, as long as it doesn't involve either party getting hurt. The point is to inject some added opportunities to bring interesting activities into your life together so that you can prevent boredom from setting in.

Yes, You Can

I'm sure some of you reading these suggestions are saying to yourself, "I could never bring myself to do something like that." If this thought is prompted not because you really don't want to role-play, but rather because you believe that you could never work up the courage, then let me see if I can help. Consider that when actors are preparing for a role, they rehearse. You can do the same thing. Put some glasses and a bottle of wine at your dining room table and pretend it's a bar and don your roles. Maybe you'll still be too nervous to pull it off the first time, but by the second or third occasion when you pretend to be this role you've chosen, I'm sure you'll start feeling more comfortable. And if you know you're going to do this, you can also rehearse by yourself. If you're driving alone in the car, talk to yourself in the role you've chosen. Or while you're taking a shower, instead of singing, rehearse your role. The more comfortable you are with this role, the easier you'll find it when acting it out with your partner. And after you've rehearsed it a few times, I believe you'll be ready to take it on the road. And by the way, I would recommend that you go to a bar that's out of your neighborhood so that you don't meet anyone you know who might not understand what you are doing. If you're too nervous to do it someplace where people might hear, then select a nearby park and meet at a bench.

Another possibility for role-playing is to pretend you're two people from the past, like Napoleon and Josephine, instead of being contemporary people. You can study their real history and use those facts in your dialogue. In a case like that, I definitely don't think you should meet in a bar, unless it's a noisy one where no one else can hear you talking about the battle of Waterloo as if it happened yesterday.

Role-playing like this is not going to be for everyone, but if you can't seem to find anything to do that will add some excitement to your relationship, then I suggest you try out an idea like this even if you don't think you'll like it. If you remain in your rut because nothing suits you, then I'd advise you to adopt one of the ideas I've presented or create your own. You have nothing to lose and a world of discovery to explore.

Secret 6

Remember the Romance

The vast majority of people, especially those who are part of a couple, understand the meaning of love because they've experienced that emotion. But romance seems to be a word that's not as well understood, particularly by men. Since romance is a requirement for a strong relationship, it is necessary to learn what romance is and how to create it.

So what is my definition of romance? To me it's the atmosphere in which love exists. If two fish were going to get together, they'd need water to swim toward each other and meet. Without that water, they'd flop around on the ground and die. In order for love to blossom, it requires an environment that we call romance.

Of course, when you're madly in love, everything and anything can be romantic. Take the song from the musical *My Fair Lady* titled "On the Street Where You Live," in which the man waxes romantic about the street where his loved one lives, though to anyone else it's just a street. At that stage in a relationship, romance sort of takes care of itself.

Some men have figured out that if the woman of their dreams isn't in love with them, by creating as romantic an atmosphere as possible, they can ignite that spark of love in her.

Not every man is able to overwhelm the object of his desire the way Tony did, but no matter how a couple starts off their relationship, in most cases, the intense emotions can begin to fade a

CASE HISTORY *Tony and Donna*

Donna met Tony at a party. She was twenty-one and he was a dozen years older. She was second-generation Italian American and he was newly arrived from Italy. They shared some cultural aspects, but on other levels they were far apart. Donna didn't think that their meeting at the party had any significance, but Tony decided that he'd met his wife. To make his dream come true, Tony launched a romantic campaign. Donna received roses almost daily. When the deliveryman wasn't carrying flowers, it was a box of chocolates. And the mailman almost always brought with him a letter, or two, filled with romantic thoughts. After he'd persuaded Donna to go out with him, he'd take her to the most romantic restaurants and treat her like a queen. Soon enough, Donna forgot about their difference in age and got used to having Italian operas played on his car stereo. Within a year they were married and not long after that, had their first bambino.

few years into the relationship unless you actively work at reviving them. So adding a dose of romance into your life becomes critical to keeping the relationship healthy. For romantic gestures to have the proper effect on a woman, they must be initiated by the man, and that means that men have to learn what they can do to improve their skills in this arena.

Don't allow the romance of your relationship to diminish as your years together add up.

Romance in the Bedroom

The first secret of adding romance to your relationship is to think of your partner first. With regard to your sex life, make a point of discovering what your partner would like and make sure that from this moment on, his or her desires, assuming you don't find them repulsive, are part of your sexual repertoire. Making sacrifices for your partner is definitely romantic, though when it comes to sex, adding a particular technique should be something you'll both enjoy.

CASE HISTORY *Ted and Mary*

Ted and Mary got married on Valentine's Day and because their tenth anniversary was approaching, Ted knew that he had to come up with something special. Dinner in a nice restaurant didn't seem special enough, so Ted kept racking his brain for something better. Then he saw an ad for a nearby hotel that had fixed up some of its rooms for lovers, adding mirrors on the ceiling and a special chair for having sex. Ted reserved one, and at a hefty price because the rates spiked on Valentine's Day. When he brought Mary there that night, instead of being delighted, she cried.

Ted had made the classic mistake of equating kinky sex with romance. Of course he wasn't alone, which is why the motel was able to charge more on Valentine's Day, and there are certainly women who love to have wild sex and would like to spend a few hours in a room like that. But for Mary this wasn't just a Valentine's Day but the tenth anniversary of their wedding, a day she had spent years dreaming about before she walked down that aisle and which still filled her with wonderful feelings when she thought back on it. A cheesy motel room decked out like a brothel was not the environment for celebrating this sacred day in their life together.

Where to Begin

While a romantic interlude possibly will wind up in the bedroom, it's not likely to start there. Romance is delicate and needs to have a gentle start. You have to prepare the way for romance, so let me give you some advice on how best to do that. Admittedly, I'm writing mostly for my male audience.

What to Wear

Let's start with the dress code. If you're looking to set a romantic atmosphere, begin with your wardrobe. For example, if you're planning a romantic date and there's a choice between two activities, one of which requires the two of you to dress up somewhat and the other of which allows for slouchy clothes, the one that requires an effort to look neat is the more romantic. Why is that, you might ask? Because it shows you care. Does that mean going on a hike together wearing shorts and T-shirts can't be romantic? Of course not, but on the other hand, if you're going out for dinner and one restaurant insists on a certain dress code, not necessarily formal, and the other allows shorts and T-shirts, then it's the former that is the more romantic venue. Because you've chosen that restaurant, it means that you're going to invest more in the evening by getting dressed up, and that makes it more romantic.

You don't have to agree with this observation. Many men may not feel more romantic wearing a pair of slacks than a pair of jeans, but most women will agree with me, and so that's just the way it is and you might as well accept it.

*The better you dress, the more romantic
the atmosphere.*

Set the Atmosphere

Atmosphere is another ingredient. Harsh light shows off faults while soft light hides them. Women spend a lot of time looking at their faults in the mirror. They're very conscious of them, as are some men. Reducing those worries makes her feel more at ease, and so soft light is more romantic. Whether it be a restaurant with the lights turned down low or a candlelit bedroom or a hot tub under the stars, making the effort to choose the right lighting can pay off.

I understand that there are men who would much prefer to have the lights turned way up, especially in that hot tub scenario. Men like to look at their partner's body and so the more light there is, the better the view. But if a woman has to worry about every flaw she has, real or perceived, then that's going to be quite a distraction and she's not going to feel very sexy.

There are other ways you can create a romantic setting in addition to the lighting. Flowers offer both visual and aromatic romantic signals. You can also add romantic scents via certain candles or by burning incense.

Pay attention to the atmosphere when trying to create a romantic setting.

What to Say

If what you wear and the lighting has an effect on romance, without a doubt what you say is a critical factor also. You can't be romantic all the time, but there are times when you have to remember to "whisper sweet nothings." Conversely, you also have to keep in mind that if you use harsh words, they will have an effect long after they've left your lips.

And don't forget that if your efforts at communicating romance are boring, they're not going to be very romantic. If you merely mouth the words "I love you" once a day before you hit the pillow, that sentiment is going to lose much of its punch. So you have to vary the times you say it, and even the words you use. You have to put some energy into this process. If you find it easier to do this in writing, and leave little love notes around, that's fine. Just keep in mind that any way you communicate your love to your partner is going to have a positive effect as long as you put some effort and imagination into it.

It's also important that romantic communication occur regularly, especially not just when you want to have sex, timing that will only backfire. Again, these should be heartfelt, not empty words. Presumably, you do feel lovingly toward your partner during the course of the day, and all I'm suggesting is that you share those emotions. And these days there are so many ways to communicate that you really have no excuse. Just be careful what you say in an e-mail, since employers may be reading incoming e-mail messages.

Body Language

There are societies where the women are supposed to walk several steps behind husbands when they are in public. I can't imagine that such marriages are very romantic. In our society there are no rules like this, but if a couple voluntarily gives each other signs of affection, both in public and private, like holding hands or putting their arms around each other, such open declarations of their love are definitely romantic.

One of the reasons why such signs are romantic is because they are proof that you know that your partner is there at your side. You are paying attention to each other rather than acting as two separate entities who happen to be near each other. And the more such positive connections there are between the two of you, the more romance is added to your relationship. Every time you touch you'll get a small spark, and those in turn will charge up your relationship.

At this point I'd like to mention a type of body language that has the opposite effect and will sap the electricity out of a relationship faster than greased lightning, and that's when a man walking along with his partner checks out other women, especially if he's very obvious about it. Any woman is going to be hurt by such ogling and it completely deflates the romance of the moment. Yet, sadly, I hear about such behavior far too often. I understand that if a sexy woman who's half undressed walks by, any man is going to sneak a peek. But a peek is not staring with your mouth hanging open.

Romantic Gestures

If you love someone, it should go without saying that you care about this person. And if you care about someone, you want to minimize any burdens they may have, so if you're being a couch potato and you see your partner walking by carrying a big pile of laundry, you should get up and offer your assistance. Maybe your assistance won't be needed and you'll be told that you can sit back down on that couch, but just offering is a romantic gesture because it's proof that you do care.

Habits That Drive Your Partner Crazy

When two people live together, it's impossible to constantly be on your best behavior. But some people develop habits that are so repetitive that they don't give romance an opportunity to put down any roots. Here's what I mean: nose picking, belching, passing gas, slurping, and so on. Sometimes it's unavoidable, but at least make sure you excuse yourself. Also, there's a difference between the occasional belch when it can't be helped, and making absolutely no effort to contain them, or even forcing out every possible belch. These habits are not romantic, are not sexy, and after a while are quite annoying. When your partner expects you to belch after every gulp of soda, then each of those belches is going to be extra annoying because of their repetition, which will have a very negative effect on your love life as well as your social life.

Being part of a couple means being considerate of the other person. It also means being reasonable. Habits that can be annoying can also include acting unreasonably. It's okay to want the place where you live to be neat, but if you're too neat, that can make it hard for your partner to enjoy the space you share. So if you tend to take some things to the extreme, be it neatness or sloppiness, then you have to understand that this is going to have a negative impact on your relationship.

Taking Romance on the Road

Boredom can definitely make it harder for romance to thrive. If you can predict what your partner is going to do when you're together down to the second, then even gestures that should be considered romantic will lose much of their effect. But it can be hard to change a routine when you're always in the same surroundings. Sometimes in order to make romance bloom, you have to take it out for some fresh air.

Ideally this romantic trip should be to a vacation paradise for two luxurious weeks, but your schedule and pocketbook may limit where you go. The point is to get out of your normal environment where the air has become stale. Even if the change is just to four different walls, hopefully there will be a positive effect. I say "hopefully" because both parties have to bring along a willingness to allow for some changes. Potentially you can bring your rut with you, and if that's the case, it can spoil the effects of even the most luxurious getaways. But if you bring an open mind with you, as well as an active imagination, then I would hope you could make some headway no matter your destination.

One of the reasons a trip can be more romantic than staying at home is that the long list of chores that are always looming on the home front, as well as work assignments, can be more easily blocked from your conscience when they're physically not present.

Some people avoid taking an extended vacation because of the pile of work that has to be faced when they return to their desks. If you spend all your vacation time worrying about this growing pile, that is going to dampen the romantic atmosphere, but you can, and should, put this worry out of your mind. Everyone needs to recharge the batteries now and then, and whether you realize it or not, if you have no expectations of ever getting any time off, it's going to effect the quality of your work. So while vacations should be romantic, they also serve other purposes. And the expectation of an upcoming vacation can also do wonders for your love life. Knowing that there will be a block of time set aside for the two of you to spend together romantically can help you keep that flame of romance alive even during the days/weeks/months when you can't really attend to it.

Plan on taking time away from home to increase the romance in your relationship.

Just because you're off on vacation doesn't automatically mean that it's going to be all that romantic. You may be having sex more often, but you still need to work on making your vacation romantic. All it really takes is to stay focused on each other: to spend time taking walks while holding each other; stopping every once in a while to nuzzle; smiling at each other; doing silly things to entertain each other; maybe doing some of those sexy exercises I mentioned earlier; stopping into an empty bar in the middle of the day and canoodling in the booth at the back over a couple of drinks; lying in each other's arms in the hammock on the porch; giving each other a massage with scented oils; picking wildflowers; feeding each other grapes; reading poems or maybe a chapter of my favorite book, *Lady Chatterley's Lover*, to each other; sitting next to each other watching the sun set or getting up early to watch it rise or lying on a blanket at night, counting shooting stars.

No matter how long a list of romantic activities I could give you, I still might be missing one or two that your partner finds very romantic. Since you can't guess what your partner feels is romantic, you have to ask. I would suggest that you don't do it while you're on vacation but way ahead of time. That way you can take whatever proactive steps might be necessary to include those romantic activities, like purchasing tickets to a concert or bringing along a certain type of music, of an artist or genre your partner finds particularly romantic.

Time to Go Home

Since all good things come to an end, soon enough you'll be back home, following the same old routines. But it is possible to continue the effects of your vacation into your daily life, even if only in a subtle manner. Let me give you some suggestions of how to do this.

If your trip was to some tropical isle where you had piña coladas every afternoon, then why not buy some piña colada mix and make some for yourselves every now and then? This will bring back some of the memories of your trip and serve to further ingrain those romantic moments in your memory banks. (And of course the alcohol might put you into a more romantic mood as well.)

Once a week you could make a point of going to a restaurant that specializes in the type of food from the place you visited.

Assuming you took lots of pictures, blow some of them up and put them around the house where you can see them. If photos are buried in an album you never look at, they will trigger memories only when you bother to take it out. But if they're put out for regular viewing, they can evoke happy memories over and over again. If you took digital pictures, there are now electronic frames that will display your pictures in a continuous slide show on your computer.

While you're on your trip, make a point of buying some decorative item to display in your home. Then whenever you look at it, you'll be reminded of your romantic vacation.

While you're on your travels, give yourselves new nicknames. Then when you use those names back at home, memories of your trip will come flooding back.

Try to keep the romance of your vacation alive by employing various methods to trigger memories of your time away from home.

Joys of Repetition

Now I'm going to contradict what I've been telling you about doing something new by saying that repetition can be romantic too. Let's say that you have a favorite restaurant you both find romantic. Obviously, you shouldn't go there every night, but if you go once a month, you won't turn it into a boring evening but can use it as a romantic oasis instead. The same is true for vacation places. A yearly trip to the same resort can be just as romantic or more so than visiting someplace new.

One reason for this romantic effect is the anticipation you'll feel. Weeks before you take off, you'll be picturing what this upcoming vacation will be like and so you can benefit from those expectations. It will also make the memories clearer because they'll be reinforced each time you return. You won't be asking, "Do you remember the name of that little café off the main street?" Instead, you will be able to rattle off the names of many streets and places the two of you have strolled down again and again.

Everyday Romance

As hard as you may try to instill romance into a vacation, if there is little or no romance in your everyday life, then it's going to be very hard to do. I realize that if commuting and work take up most of your day, and sleep another huge chunk, it may be hard enough to fit in brushing your teeth on a daily basis without also finding a way to be romantic. But just because it might be difficult doesn't mean that you shouldn't try. Even small romantic gestures will keep the flame of your love alive so that when you do have time to really express your love, you won't be having to rub two sticks together to light the first flame.

In an earlier chapter I said that if a couple is having a hard time finding the time to have sex, they should schedule it. Here again, while I know that romance is something many people expect to spontaneously leap out of their partner whenever he or she spots you coming, the fact is that the pulls of everyday life can make spontaneous romance difficult to achieve. And so instead of waiting endlessly for that boat to the tunnel of love to pull up next to you, I'm telling you to go out of your way to create romance in your life. For example, make it a habit to touch each other as much as possible. If you're both on the couch and he's reading the paper and she's reading a book, sit closer, or share an ottoman so at least your feet are touching. I know that at that moment the material you're reading may have your attention hooked, but not so much that you can't also reach out and touch your partner. Seek out the opportunity to act as a couple rather than allow the opportunities to slip by.

Just in case you lack imagination, here are some other ways to integrate romance into your daily life:

- When you brush your teeth before going to bed, each partner should give a light shoulder rub to the other while they're brushing. (Repeat in the morning if schedules permit.) Don't just give each other a peck when you're leaving in the morning, but reserve at least thirty seconds for a good hug.

- Create an evening ritual, like a nine o'clock cup of tea together. If it becomes something that's built into the schedule, you'll tend not to put it aside so easily. And if one person has a favorite show that starts at nine on Tuesdays and the other on Wednesdays, then one of you make the tea for the other and share it while watching together for a time.

- You can even make the mundane romantic. If it's time to empty and fill the dishwasher, do it together and make sure that you "accidentally" keep bumping into each other. If you work at it, I'm sure you can figure out how to make other daily chores romantic too.

- You can even do romantic things when you're not together. Let's say the veggie bin in your fridge is a mess and you know it will drive your partner nuts. Take ten minutes to clean out the drawer, grab a sticky note and scribble a heart on it, then stick it onto the spick-and-span drawer. Believe me when I tell you it will be appreciated as a loving and romantic gesture.

Gift Giving

The people who market flowers, cards, jewelry, and especially diamonds do a good job of convincing the public that giving one of these is romantic. Of course, everyone likes to receive gifts, but whether or not a gift is a romantic gesture depends on the circumstances.

The real point of a romantic gift, and really of any gift, is to show that you are thinking of the person you're giving the gift to and that you care for him or her. Now let's say a husband has forgotten to buy his wife a gift for her birthday and anniversary. Suddenly Christmas rolls around and he buys her a diamond to make up for his neglect the rest of the year. Is his wife going to look at this diamond as a romantic gesture or a sign of guilt, making her remember once again the pain she felt when he forgot to mark all those other important days?

Most people have to live within a budget, so it shouldn't be how much a gift costs that matters. To break your budget may cause so much worry that it negates the romantic effect, and the romantic quotient comes from the thought that went into its purchase anyway. So as long as you don't just dash into the nearest flower shop or cigar store on your way home but think carefully about what your partner might enjoy, whatever gift you choose will be romantic (that is unless you give only useful appliances that remind your partner of work, not love).

And don't forget the point I made earlier with reference to gifts for women, that is, that sending a gift like flowers ahead of time will have more of a romantic effect. Since women take a longer time to get aroused, flowers received in the morning are a lot more effective at exciting her libido than those brought to the door that evening.

When Romance Is Boring

I'm sure you've experienced hearing someone say thank you in a monotone as compared to someone else who said it with a big smile. Yes, the person in the first case was being polite, but you can tell he or she didn't really mean it, which lowers the value of what they expressed quite a bit.

The same effect can occur with regard to romantic gestures that are said or done by rote. Your partner can tell when your heart isn't really in it, and so rather than being romantic the words end up having little positive or even a negative effect.

So if you say "I love you" even when you're very busy, for those few seconds put your emotions into what you are saying. Your partner is the most important person in the world to you, so isn't he or she worth the extra effort? I recognize that there are times when we are so deeply involved with something that we don't want to spoil our concentration by switching focus. That can happen every once in a while, but if it's happening every time you say something that's supposed to be romantic, then you're sending just the opposite message.

The same applies to other romantic gestures. A dinner in a restaurant can be romantic but only if the two of you are concentrating on each other, not focused on the food. And flowers are wonderful, but not if they're always roses. You have to use your imagination in every aspect of your relationship if you're going to be successful at creating a romantic atmosphere.

Secret 7

Afterplay Is as Important as Foreplay

In this chapter I want to go into more detail about afterplay because it's a term, and more important, an activity that gets far too little attention. In fact, I believe the vast majority of people have never heard of it, though every woman will instantly know what I'm talking about when she reads this.

The sexual response of men and women is different. You know that, I'm sure. Men get aroused faster and lose their arousal much quicker too, once they've had an orgasm. (In young men, that's not always true because some of them can have an orgasm and maintain an erection, or must wait only moments to have a new one and keep going. But such sexual energy doesn't last forever.) Women, in general, take longer to become aroused, and then after they've had an orgasm, it also takes them longer to come down from the aroused state. If it helps you to picture this as a graph, a man's arousal curve is very steep, forming a narrow upside-down V, while a woman's is much more gradual, both on the upswing and on the way back down, closer to the classic bell curve.

So if a man rolls over and goes right to sleep after reaching orgasm, he's leaving his partner in the lurch. At that point she is craving to be caressed and cuddled, and instead she's left with a dead weight lying next to her with her needs for affection unfulfilled. And it's the satisfying of those needs that we call afterplay.

Most men have now learned to give their wives foreplay because they've come to realize that the better lovers they are, meaning the better they are at giving their partners sexual satisfaction, the more likely their partners are to want sex. Even among men who might prefer to have the entire sexual episode over and done with in a matter of minutes, most now know that they have to lengthen the process so that their partner enjoys it too. They accept that they have to put off their own sexual gratification in order to help their partner climb that bell curve so she can become sufficiently aroused to have an orgasm. Among the success stories in all the media coverage of sex is that the days of slam, bam, thank you, ma'am are just about over.

But the same can't be said of afterplay. Far too many men ignore this time period, short as it may be. And far too many women crave afterplay but don't know that this is natural. So they don't ask their partners to become as expert in afterplay as they are, hopefully, at foreplay.

CASE HISTORY Kevin and Rachel

Rachel considered Kevin to be a very good lover. He knew exactly what to do to make her body aroused and only when she was just about to have an orgasm did he begin intercourse so that she almost always came away satisfied, and sometimes they even managed to have their orgasms simultaneously.

However, as soon as Kevin had his orgasm, no matter whether they'd made love at night or during the afternoon on a weekend, he'd turn over, curl up into a ball and fall asleep. A few times Rachel had complained to Kevin about this, but he'd always responded that he couldn't stop himself.

Rachel ended up having strong feelings of abandonment because of this and after a while, to avoid these feelings, she began to avoid having sex with Kevin. She didn't make a conscious decision to turn down his requests for sex because she knew she wouldn't get any afterplay; instead, the negative reaction toward sex was more instinctual. Getting turned down with greater and greater frequency made Kevin angry and their entire relationship began to grow distant. That's when they came to see me and I was able to piece together what was occurring in their love life.

While it may appear that what happened to Kevin and Rachel was a bit extreme, if you think of a relationship as being like a sweater, and understand that one little thread coming undone can cause the whole garment to fall apart, then it makes more sense. Especially when all this plays out in a couple's sex life. As I've said, sex is the glue that keeps a relationship together, so if a couple's sex life gets damaged, the entire relationship can come undone.

A Quickie

It's very important for you to understand that afterplay does not have to extend anywhere near as long as foreplay. A few minutes should do the trick. And for a man to say that he is so sleepy he can't pay attention to his partner for a few minutes more is absurd. Just think of afterplay as a quickie for her.

Some men act this way because they resent foreplay. They say to themselves, "I performed foreplay for the necessary time, which was for her benefit, so now she can do me the favor of just letting me go to sleep." Obviously, this isn't a very loving attitude, is it? If sex has lasted under thirty minutes in its entirety, what's another couple of minutes? It should be nothing, but it seems that it is too much for some men.

I once received a letter from a man who said that the only way he could get to sleep was to have sex and then fall right to sleep. If he didn't follow that routine, he would be up half the night. So this man gets a pass. But not the rest of you! Maybe I can convince you with logic, even if I can't force you.

Assuming you now understand the benefits of foreplay, I'm here to tell you that afterplay should really be considered part of foreplay. I'm not saying that you're going to go back to having sex immediately afterward. What I am saying is that the benefits of afterplay, the way it works in the woman's mind, will carry over to the next time you have sex. If your partner has a completely satisfying sexual experience from beginning to end, then you can understand why she would be more eager to repeat it. However, if she's left with a bad taste in her mouth because the very end of the experience didn't meet her expectations, that's going to carry over until the next time, or should I say potential next time, comes along. And remember, this probably won't be a conscious decision. She won't be saying to herself, "I'm angry that I didn't get any afterplay the last time so I'm going to withhold sex." Her reaction will just be "Sex isn't so great so I can't be bothered."

Permit me to illustrate this effect with an example. Let's say you go to a restaurant and have a great meal, but then the waiter disappears and it takes twenty minutes for you to pay your check. The next time you're going out to dinner and you think of that restaurant, instead of saying to yourself what a great meal you had the last time you were there, you're going to remember the frustration you felt trying to pay the bill, and so you may choose to dine elsewhere.

The above situation is similar to what happens when your partner thinks of the last time she had sex with you. Instead of remembering the fabulous orgasm you gave her, she'll recall that at the end she felt disappointed that you abandoned her in her moment of need. On the other hand, if you do a good job at afterplay, and hold her and caress her and tell her how much you love her for a few moments, then instead of feeling disappointed, she'll feel all warm and glowing. And those feelings will carry over to the next time the subject of having sex comes around.

Yes, that's right, if you do a good job at afterplay, it will actually be the start of foreplay for the next time you have sex, even if it's days or even a week later. Whenever you begin, your partner will think back to the last time and her mind will be flooded with positive feelings. That will make her arousal proceed even faster. So for all you male bean counters out there, what I'm saying is that the minutes you spend in afterplay may save you even more time as your partner will become fully aroused in fewer minutes the next time. And more important, the next time may arrive somewhat sooner too.

Keep in mind that, if the last time you made love was not one of your best performances, she may still have been completely satisfied because you did a good job at afterplay. It's that last impression that may carry over the next time you bring up the subject of sex. Potentially, excellence at afterplay can raise a B+ in lovemaking for one session to an overall A.

How to Be a Good Afterplayer

Since men don't appreciate afterplay, one reaction to such a request might be, "I don't know what it is, so how can I do it?" Since it's so simple, it won't take much to explain.

What men have to get through their thick skulls, oops, I mean understand, is that after a woman has an orgasm, she's still aroused. She doesn't have a penis that quickly goes flaccid. Her entire vaginal area is engorged with blood and it takes a while for it to dissipate. In actuality, it's not so much what the man does that's important, but that he *be* there while her arousal is going down. And by *be* I don't mean sleeping next to her. He has to be conscious. And to prove to her he's conscious, he should simply kiss her gently, caress her a bit, hug her, and say "I love you." There's no magic formula. She just needs to be with her lover during this time.

By the way, I've been accusing men of falling asleep because that is a common occurrence. If he gets up out of bed and leaves the room, that's not any better, and might even be worse if he leaves and doesn't come back. And if he reaches for the remote and turns on the TV, that's not good either.

Ill-Timed Bathroom Break

There are some women who are guilty of killing the opportunity for afterplay. As soon as their partner has ejaculated, they get out of bed to wash up. They are so afraid that any of his ejaculate seeping out of her vagina will dirty the sheets that they're willing to give up on afterplay in order to maintain cleanliness.

While you're probably not going to find the male partners of such women picketing on their front lawns, the fact is that it's both members of the couple who are suffering when she makes a mad dash for the bathroom. Even if her desire to clean up is stronger than her need for afterplay, she still has a need for afterplay. If she gives in to the call of the bidet, or whatever method she uses to clean up, when she looks back at the last time she had sex, that memory won't have the proper warm and fuzzy glow. She'll be thinking "big mess" and that's not going to do much for her level of arousal.

Any woman who has this compulsion should be prepared. She should have a towel nearby and maybe even before she and her partner begin sex, she should put it under her, or at the very least have it ready for when they're done. Or have a box of tissues at hand that she can use to blot any seepage. That way she won't have to worry that anything dripping out of her vagina is going to dirty the sheets and she can lie there and bask in the glow of afterplay.

It was suggested to me by one gentleman that the reason women are getting less afterplay is that fewer and fewer people are smoking. There was a time when an aftersex smoke was automatic, and the two partners would lie there in each other's arms, enveloped by the smoke from the cigarettes. That may be so, though it's not an excuse for couples to take up this nasty habit. But acknowledging this change might offer couples an alternative when seeking a replacement for the postlovemaking cigarette. For example, more and more people are drinking bottled water. Perhaps if you placed a couple of bottles of water next to the bed before making love, afterward you could share a moment drinking from them. Or else you could substitute something else to drink. Or you could have some grapes and feed them to each other. Or rub some cream on each other. Or there could be a wet washcloth with which he could clean her vagina. There are any number of possibilities, but if it takes having a routine in order to integrate afterplay into your love life, then by all means figure out together what that might be for the two of you.

Don't forget to remain consciously together for a few moments after orgasm.

Of course, while afterplay is important, there are going to be times when it's going to be skipped. Just as it's better to take your time making love but doesn't mean you can't have a quickie now and then, there are going to be times when afterplay doesn't fit in. That's fine, as long as you both understand that it is an exception rather than the rule.

Secret 8

Improve Communication

I've given you some secrets on how to improve your love life, but having secrets to follow won't help you make progress in improving your love life if you're not communicating properly. Most of these secrets are only effective if the two of you are sharing your thoughts and feelings, at least to some extent. Couples may not need to be constantly joined at the hip for these secrets to work, but you have to come together more often than when you're having sex, and for that to happen, you need to be exchanging your ideas and feelings on a regular basis. Additionally, these secrets I've given you are guidelines more than hard and fast rules. The two of you have to figure out how to fit them into your own life as a couple. Again, you can't do that if you're each living in a parallel universe. You have to be talking and listening to each other in order to make these secrets effective. So in this chapter I'm going to give you some lessons on how to communicate so that you can follow this secret:

Work at remaining connected through good communication.

Stripping Minds and Bodies

When you sit down to ponder the relationships of couples who have problems talking to each other about their sexual needs, you can't help but conclude that it's a little strange that two people can take off all their clothes in front of each other, engage in intimate acts, have orgasms together, and yet not be able to speak to each other about the very acts they have just performed. I don't know enough about how the brain works to state this conclusively, but it's almost as if we humans have split personalities on some levels, at least when it comes to sex. We can be extremely intimate on a physical basis and then be almost like strangers when it comes to communicating verbally about what we do together physically. If the subject matter is about what needs to be put on the grocery list, most people don't have any difficulties saying what they feel. But when it comes to what sexual acts to put on the bedroom headboard list, then suddenly we get all tongue-tied. Perhaps all this stems from the days of early man, when sex was required for procreation but man's linguistic skills were far less developed. Back in those days, sex was a need that had to be sated, not talked about. But today, we've advanced in how we go about having sex, perhaps more so than in our ability to communicate on the subject.

One reason for this dichotomy between doing and talking stems from how much more invested we are in our sexual feelings than in how we feel about other aspects of our lives, like buying groceries. For example, let's say a man wanted to add anal sex to the couple's sexual repertoire. He would instinctively know that it isn't like asking for another six-pack of beer to be thrown into the shopping cart. He would understand that there is a risk attached to this request, that by bringing up the subject of anal sex, not only might he face rejection, but his partner might actually get upset at him for bringing up such a concept. The potential for total rejection would certainly raise the stakes of the request, maybe to the point of making it a topic to avoid rather than pursue.

Life-Threatening Silence

To prove my point that we tend to avoid talking about some matters when the risk of rejection is high, this type of avoidance takes place even when keeping quiet could have life-threatening consequences. Sadly, many people who have a sexually transmitted disease, including HIV-AIDS, won't reveal the state of their health to a potential sex partner out of fear of being rejected. And how many people who are STD free actually raise the subject either? They'd rather hope that a potential partner doesn't have an STD than ask this person to get tested, even though as a consequence of their silence, they might become infected. Unfortunately, it's because people can't find a way to express themselves when it comes to sexually transmitted diseases (even if they'll talk about another medical condition so much you can't stand it) that these diseases have become so widespread.

Fortunately, with regard to talking about STDs, the need for this type of communication has become somewhat less vital. That's because condom usage has become so much more commonplace that people who are having sex for the first time don't have to talk about using them, but instead both individuals just assume that a condom will be part of the program. Of course, if they could talk about condom usage, then they could also communicate their other sexual needs. But here we're talking about people first having sex, and that's not your case at all.

CASE HISTORY *Bonnie and Henry*

Bonnie and Henry had been married for two years. Their sex life, which in the beginning had been very passionate, had begun to decline, both in frequency and variety. One day Henry decided to take things into his own hands. He went to a store that sold X-rated DVDs and purchased a copy of the classic porno film

Deep Throat. Henry hadn't seen many porno films, but he had seen this one at a frat party and thought that it was more humorous than sexy and so might be fun to watch together, as well as add some spice to their sex life. That night he started the DVD and told Bonnie to come watch. As soon as Bonnie saw what was on the screen, she ran out of the room and locked herself in the bedroom.

Getting Your Message Across

This was a case of miscommunication. Perhaps Bonnie would have been willing to watch a porno film if she'd agreed to it ahead of time and if they'd talked about the reason he wanted to watch that particular one. By springing this as a surprise, she assumed that he was trying to get her to perform deep throat oral sex on him. She did perform oral sex, but she hated the idea of having to put his entire penis in her mouth, and it was this miscommunication that caused her to get so upset. So because Henry hadn't talked about this with her ahead of time, he compounded his mistake and it took more than a week before they had sex again, and it was over a month before Bonnie would agree to any kind of oral sex.

There are many ways of causing a miscommunication. Having good communication doesn't mean that you can say whatever pops into your head, but rather that you share information in such a way that both points of view are heard and digested. If you speak or act too gruffly or forcefully, you may get the opposite reaction to the one you seek.

Be very careful about the messages you give when talking about your sex life.

Only the Beginning

When talking about touchy subjects, and we agree that sex is one of those, every word carries extra meaning. Which is why it's a good idea to think about what was just said before reacting. If your partner lays something on the table concerning your sex life, you may feel that you have to respond immediately but not only isn't there a rule that says you must, in many cases I'd advise you to think before you speak. Certainly there'll be other opportunities for the two of you to talk. So if a subject is brought up by your partner that takes you by surprise, don't be in such a rush to answer. Instead, say that you need some time to think about it, and do just that. If you say the first thing that pops into your head, you might say the wrong thing. So don't be afraid to be a little cautious. You'll undoubtedly have to negotiate a bit in order to come to an understanding you can both find acceptable so don't rush to answer a question you feel uncomfortable with until you've had a chance to properly think it through.

Start by Listening

Communication is a two-way street involving a back-and-forth exchange of information, especially between lovers. And that "information" is not limited to the words that are used. The tone in which those words are spoken can be just as important. The body language of the person speaking, as well as that of the listener, also plays a role. Another factor is whether both parties are equally engaged or whether one is monopolizing the conversation.

If you are going to raise an important topic, it is vital to get a feel for your companion's attitude before you bring up any points that are likely to stir the pot. If you're addressing the topic of making changes to your sex life, you'd better make certain that your partner is in the right frame of mind to be receptive to such suggestions. If your partner is frazzled, distracted, angry, depressed or nervous, that is not the time to raise an issue that is likely to intensify any negative emotions your partner may already be experiencing. And the only way to discover the true nature of your lover's emotional state is to begin the conversation on a simple note and listen carefully to his or her response.

Learn to read your partner's moods.

If you can't tell from your partner's response how he or she is feeling, then may I suggest that you take some lessons in human behavior? People give many different clues to their emotions when they talk and it shouldn't be that hard to figure out your partner's emotional state. Of course, there's always the direct approach, which is to ask "How are you feeling?" and then listen carefully to the answer. If it appears that your partner may not be receptive to what you were thinking of discussing, then put the discussion off to another time. Assuming this is a topic you've been pondering for quite a while, a few more days, or even weeks, won't much matter.

CASE HISTORY Mary Jane and Jay

Mary Jane read for the umpteenth time in one of her women's magazines that every woman has a right to have orgasms. She'd been faking them for years and as she put the magazine down, she said to herself, *Now is the time to tell Jay.* Jay was in the kitchen. His head was under the sink because he was installing a new water purifier they'd just bought. Seeing Jay like that actually gave Mary Jane courage. Since she couldn't see his face, she felt more comfortable telling him that for the ten years of their marriage, she'd been faking orgasms. She began by asking him how it was going. He said, "Fine," but he was grunting from the effort of separating two pipes that had been joined together for thirty years. Those grunts might have given her an indication that he wasn't as fine as he'd reported, but Mary Jane decided to go forward and said to him, "Jay, I just wanted to tell you that for the last ten years, I've been faking my orgasms." Jay's response to this was again, "Fine." Mary Jane was so upset that she kicked his leg and ran out of the kitchen. Upon being kicked, Jay raised his head and bumped it against a pipe. He lay there for a while, wondering what had just happened, and then went back to work.

One human quirk many of us share when we have something to say that we feel is important is that as we're speaking, we tend not to listen to the other person. Our heads are so filled with our train of thought and we're concentrating so hard on getting the words out that we don't always stop to see how the other person is reacting. Maybe we've only barely begun to formulate our argument and we're then so worried about what we're going to say next that we don't listen to what's being "said" in response to our first statement. (I put the word *said* in quotation marks because it could be a verbal response or just as likely a message conveyed with body language, such as a frown or a smile.) We may even become annoyed that the person we're talking to has interrupted, though he or she may yet have no idea that this is a topic of such importance to us. Not stopping to assess the reaction to your initial statements is a big mistake, especially when the topic has to do with your shared sex life, in which both viewpoints carry equal weight.

Of course in our case, Mary Jane made every mistake in the book. In fact, she would have had a hard time picking a worse moment to bring up the subject of their sex life. But she'd been stewing over this issue for years, and when the magazine article finally gave her the courage to speak up, she didn't want to miss the opportunity. To her, having her husband under the sink, where he couldn't move or give her a nasty look, seemed perfect. The only good thing about it was that he hadn't been paying attention to her words, and as far as he was concerned it never happened, so Mary Jane was free to try again, hopefully at a more opportune time.

If the mood isn't right, don't bring up a sensitive subject.

A Negative Reaction

If upon hearing your proposal, your partner's face turns into a frown, or maybe even a scowl, then rather than continuing to press on with your request, you have to put it back on the shelf. This is not a debate where you hope to impress the audience by overwhelming your opposition with facts. This is about personal opinions where you can both be right. What you want might be quite reasonable to you, but that doesn't mean that your partner has to agree.

For example, even if every other couple in the world is performing oral sex, your partner still has a right to say no. You can't pressure people into adopting new sexual positions. Since it involves the pleasure of both partners, both partners have to accept or reject it.

I have to admit that sometimes a person will change her or his mind. Maybe a specific argument might work, or pleading might win the day. But there also might be a price to pay for being too persistent. Your partner may end up resenting this pressure and avoid having sex with you altogether, at least for a time. So that's why you have to listen for clues. You have to be extra sensitive when it comes to figuring out what your partner is really saying, as well as feeling, so that you don't cross some line that will lead to negative consequences for your overall relationship.

Controlling Electronics

In order to listen to what your partner has to say, you have to give him or her your full concentration. If there is a lot of background noise, that's going to be difficult to do. And that's particularly so if the noise is coming from a TV, which will add to the confusion by also distracting your eyes. So when having a serious conversation, turn off all electronic equipment, including radios, TVs, stereos, iPods and computers, or at least move to some room in the house where they all can't be heard or seen.

While I'm on this subject, let me say something about television in particular. You definitely should not have a TV in your bedroom. If every night when you go to bed you watch the evening news or a late-night comedian, you'll be missing out on sharing some important time together. If you want to watch a show, watch the show. But if you're in your bedroom, then either go to sleep or share some intimacy. Don't put your relationship at risk by having a TV competing for your attention.

And if you can afford it, I would suggest you get a TiVo or some other recording device so that you can watch your favorite shows whenever you want to watch them, not just when the networks make them available. We all have favorite shows, but they shouldn't come ahead of our partners. By recording them to watch later on, if your partner requires your attention, you can then give it without feeling that you're missing anything. As the commercials show, recording can even be done during a sports event, so there's no reason to hush your spouse during the game; instead, you can politely listen and then rewind to watch what you missed.

Leave Time for Reflection

I mentioned this point earlier, but I want to repeat it: when it comes to a sensitive subject like sex, people usually need time to reflect before responding. That may seem obvious, but if you're very eager to hear your partner agree to a request you've just made, then you might push for an immediate answer. But being pushy in such situations may lead to the opposite of what you want to happen. Let's say you brought up the idea of using a particular sexual position for the first time. If your partner has never thought about it, he or she may not be sure of how to react. The use of this position may call for some reflection of the consequences of saying yes or no. Don't assume that because your partner didn't give you an enthusiastic, affirmative reply, it means that you are being turned down. It may also mean that she or he just needs some time to think it over.

If you pressure your partner, your partner's reaction is likely going to be openly negative in order not to give in to something he or she may later regret. The more pressure you exert, the more the partner is going to dig in his or her heels. So the better tactic is not to add any pressure but allow your partner the time he or she needs to digest what you have put on the table. I would even advise you to offer them that time: "Honey, you don't have to answer me right now, just think about it, okay?" Then the next time you bring it up, you'll get a more honest answer. And at that time, if you want to try to push your point, go ahead because your partner will have had the time to think about it further and so may be more open to hearing your arguments.

And, of course, you will need some time to reflect on anything your partner may have said to you. For example, if the subject is oral sex, and your partner implies in any way that this act is "dirty," maybe the next time you talk about this you can get around that particular objection. If the two of you were to take a shower together and clean each other's genitals, any worries about your "dirty" genitals could be removed. I'm not saying that there's any guarantee that this will work, though some of my patients have had some success with the bathing technique when dealing with this objection, but I offer it to show you that you may be able to come up with a creative solution of your own. It might not be apparent before you hear your partner's objections, but upon reflection, an idea may dawn on you.

Don't be too eager to get an immediate answer.

Communication Needs to Be Regular

For communication to be effective, it has to be part of a continuum. If you and your partner rarely speak about important matters (asking to pass the ketchup doesn't count), then you can't expect that a conversation about your sex life that springs out of the blue is going to be very well received. It's likely to appear to be selfishly motivated. The idea of adding positions or going on a sexy vacation or using a sex toy is ostensibly to add to the pleasure of both partners. But if one party never shares his or her thoughts, and then comes out with a desire to change the way the couple have sex, you can be sure the other partner is going to feel this is not for their mutual pleasure.

That's not to say that people can't ask their partner for an act that is strictly for their own pleasure. Two people who are in love should be willing to do things for each other. But sex is part of the couple's overall means of communication, and if the couple aren't communicating on other fronts, then it shouldn't be surprising that suggested changes in their sex life won't be well received.

CASE HISTORY *Ellen and Peter*

Ellen had a project she had to finish at work, so she came home later than usual. What she found was her husband, Peter, ensconced in front of the TV and a dark kitchen. The first words out of his mouth weren't "How was your day?" but "What's for dinner?" This wasn't surprising to Ellen, who had seen this act before, but that didn't mean that his dumping all the cooking chores into her lap didn't make her upset. She set about preparing dinner without answering him, and you can be sure that quite a few pots and pans were banged around during the process.

Later that night Peter sidled up to her and put his arms around her. It didn't take a genius to know what he was looking for. But "it" was the last thing she was going to grant given what had occurred earlier. Both ended up going to bed very frustrated, but the saddest part was that Peter had no idea why he'd been turned down.

Your Sexual Arena

You must realize that your sexual arena is far broader than your bed. If your partner asked you to help with the housework in the morning and you refused, that's going to color how your partner reacts to your request for sex later that night. So you really have to look at good communication as a continuum that lasts 24 hours a day, 365 days a year. (Yes, 24 hours, because if one of you snores so loudly that it keeps the other partner up nights, that's a form of communication, and believe me, it's definitely going to affect your overall relationship.)

Here's another part of your sexual arena. Although I accept that no one is perfect (you're allowed to be cranky or to lose your temper once in a while, as is your partner), you can't ignore the fact that any outburst is going to have an effect on later communication. Everything that you do to each other, and for each other, will affect your sexual arena. Of course I get letters from men who say that they try as hard as they can to be romantic, caring, and loving, but still their wives won't do this or that. In the first place, their wives may be smarter than these gentlemen realize. If these gestures are recent in nature, demonstrating a seemed change in personality, and then a few days later he comes up with a request having to do with their sex life, you can be sure she's going to see through this act. So as I said, you have to examine the state of your relationship regularly and make sure that your communication is in good working order all the time, not just when you want something from your partner.

***

Don't open your mouth only when you want something. Keep the conversation going all the time

Ease on up That Road

I admit it's not easy to bring up certain subjects, but it's going to be even harder if the entire subject of sex has been off-limits for the length of your relationship. I don't want to give a science lecture here, but there is a scientific principle about inertia that says if a body is at rest, it takes a lot more energy to get it moving than the amount of energy it takes to make it move faster if it is already moving. In other words, breaking the ice is harder than picking up a conversation where you left off.

If the two of you have been having sex but not saying much about the subject, then bringing up something as delicate as trying a new sexual position is going to be that much harder. What you need to do is pave the way. It doesn't have to be anything all that weighty. The idea is to get the ball rolling. (If you're familiar with that expression, then you already know about inertia, even if you weren't familiar with the term.) For example, if the next time you have sex your partner does a little something different that you find pleasing, instead of remaining mum, speak up. Tell your partner how much you enjoyed it, either while you're making love, afterward, or even both. And then ask your partner if there is anything that he or she particularly enjoyed. Or would enjoy. By making a point of communicating in the sexual arena, you'll find that it becomes easier and easier.

Noises During Sex

I don't want to skip over what can be an important part of sex, which are the noises people make, the grunts and groans, which are certainly a way of communicating enjoyment. When children hear the types of sounds lovemaking can produce coming from their parents' bedroom, they may worry that one parent is hurting the other. But when adults hear those sounds coming from the motel room next door, they recognize them as denoting extreme pleasure.

Not everyone can make such noises and still enjoy sex. To some people, the act of making noise takes away from their concentration and prevents them from having an orgasm. But for those who do not have to deal with this imposed silence, I would recommend making some sounds as a means of letting your partner know how good you are feeling. Don't go out of your way to hold them back, because if you're too shy to make a few grunts or breathe heavily in the heat of the moment, then you're certainly not going to be able to have an actual conversation about sex later on. So if you haven't been making optimal use of this form of communicating, do so the next time you have sex. If your partner makes a remark about it, voilà, you've then started a verbal communication about sex.

Some parents, worried that they are going to wake up their children, who will later ask them what those noises were, try to keep as silent as possible when they have sex. That lessens your sexual enjoyment. Instead, I suggest that you put on some background music to mask the sounds. Keep the volume at a level that will allow the music to blend in with any sounds you might make so that they won't stand out.

While this is not a book on what parents should do to maintain their sex life, there is one very important point I want to state here, and that is to install a lock on your bedroom door. If by some chance the noises that arise from having sex, or anything else, wakes up the children, you don't want them barging in. A simple hook and eye will do, and you don't have to use it at other times, and you can place it high enough that children can't lock themselves in. But this little tool will give you much added comfort and confidence that your sex life remains private.

Giving Compliments

Communication is a broad subject. Sometimes it means an exchange of information, but it can also be a way of connecting with another person. For example, if your partner is wearing something new and you tell him that it is attractive, you're going to make him feel good. It doesn't really matter what you say as long as it gives your partner a warm and fuzzy feeling. The more compliments there are between the two of you, then the easier it will be to communicate about other matters. So since compliments are a form of positive communication, look for opportunities to give them.

And for you men, here's a trick that women often use that you can too. Men will often focus on the negative while women focus on the positive. So if your partner has just dressed for a party and you don't particularly like the dress she's wearing (but you know enough not to say anything negative), you can still give a compliment by focusing on her hair or her nails or some other aspect of her appearance. And by stroking her ego at this point in evening, you'll be paving the way for some more heated activities later on.

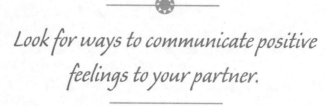

Look for ways to communicate positive feelings to your partner.

Physical Communication

Of course you can also communicate physically. A hug, a caress, a kiss, a shoulder rub are all means of communication because they are telling your partner that you love her or him. Sometimes people forget that this is a form of communication, which is why I strongly recommend using physical signs of affection as much as possible. Even if you don't feel the need for a hug at a particular moment, offering your partner one passes on the message that you're thinking about this person and that you care about him or her.

We humans actually have a need to be touched, and while there certainly is a lot of touching during sex, it's good to spread the wealth around throughout the day. Don't neglect those little touches here and there, because they mean so much.

Don't just use words to communicate, but also show signs of affection physically.

The Written Word

I'm all for sending your lover notes, letters, e-mails, and any other form of the written word. It can work especially well with regard to a touchy subject. Earlier I was saying that your partner may need some time to consider your suggestion. Making such a request in writing will allow your partner the needed time to consider your proposal before responding. It will also allow you to put your request forward in the best possible light because you can spend as much time as necessary editing your missive to make sure your meaning is very clear.

The negative side of written communication, with someone you see all the time, is that it can be seen as somewhat cold. Your partner may wonder why you didn't want to talk about this subject face-to-face. What I might suggest with regard to subjects that are a little touchy, is to drop a hint in written form—test the waters, so to speak—but not make it a formal request. For example, let's say you wanted to bring up the concept of vibrators. If you were to e-mail your partner with a link to some site on the Web about vibrators, an article or an ad, and you say "Check this out," that would let your spouse know that this was something you were interested in. Then when it came time to explore the subject, you'd do it verbally and in person. (One cautionary note: be careful what you e-mail to someone at work because employers can and do read their employees' e-mail.)

Don't Always Be Critical

There's an old saying that goes "If you can't say something nice, don't say anything at all." I understand that when you live with someone, it's probably impossible to say only nice things. There are times when you have to be critical for the other person's good. People in relationships will even rely on their partners to let them know if they're dressed oddly or don't smell as fresh as they should. And there are other times when your partner's just being annoying and you can't hold in your criticism.

However, with some couples, most of their communication is of the negative variety. If that's something they can't change, then I don't hold out much hope for their relationship. Constant carping doesn't create an environment conducive to love and sex. I recognize that there are couples who have great sex after having a big fight. I suppose it gets their adrenaline going and that's why it works. But I suspect that such fights aren't as real as they are play-acting. If through repetition you both learn that fighting leads to great sex, then you're going to fall into a routine of having fights over nothing just so you can fall into bed afterward. It's not how I would want to live my life, but if it works for these couples, fine. In such cases, both parties understand what is going on and their feelings don't get hurt because it is somewhat staged. But when someone is always saying nasty things, and meaning it, then that is not a productive form of communication.

So there's going to be a balance between compliments and criticisms in all long-term relationships. (If two people who just met are already fighting, then my advice is to part company sooner rather than later.) If you're not conscious of it, you may slide into a routine where the criticisms outnumber the compliments by a large margin. And since criticisms tend to bring out a negative attitude, your partner will probably start criticizing you in return. That can turn into a negative feedback situation where your relationship slowly spirals downward. Remember, positive feedback through all forms of communication uplifts your relationship.

Accentuate the Positive

There is one more form of criticism I want to warn you about. Let's say he says, "Let's go to the museum," and when you get there, it's closed. Or perhaps she'll bring home a sexy game and when they try it out for the first time, rather than being titillating, it's just stupid. How the two of you react to such situations is critical to the success of your program of improving communication. If you jump down each other's throats ("Why didn't you check to see if the museum was open?" "I told you that game looked stupid!"), you know what the result will be. Your partner will become gun-shy. Instead of going out of his or her way to make improvements to your relationship, just the opposite will happen. Even if a good idea pops up, rather than take a risk, your partner will push the thought aside.

So if your partner makes an effort to bring you closer together in some way, whatever the result, your job is to offer encouragement. If the museum is closed, see if there isn't a nearby art gallery that's open. Or go to the newsstand, buy an art magazine, and look it over while having a cup of coffee somewhere. Instead of giving nasty looks and saying mean things, act as a teammate would and see if you can't turn this negative into a positive. After all, you're in this relationship together. You'll get your chance to make mistakes too, so in the meantime be as supportive of your partner as you can.

CASE HISTORY *Brad and Katherine*

Katherine met a friend for coffee one Saturday afternoon and learned that there was a nearby bed-and-breakfast that had added hot tubs to many of the rooms, along with romantic decorative trimmings. It really sounded like the perfect place to spend the weekend they had planned. She got all excited thinking about it and couldn't wait to tell him. When she got home, she found Brad playing a board game with their two children. As soon as Katherine walked into the den, she said to Brad, "You know what Marissa told me? There's a new bed-and-breakfast across town that put hot tubs in some of the rooms. Wouldn't that be a great place to spend that weekend?" Brad turned to Katherine and threw her a look just as one of the children piped up, "I love hot tubs; when are we going?"

Choosing Where to Communicate

There's always a context to your communication. Part of that context is emotional. That's why I already mentioned that you need to assess your partner's mood before broaching a delicate subject to make sure he or she isn't angry or nervous. But there is also a physical context. For example, hopefully, you'd know better than Katherine did to bring up a night at a motel in front of your children. Or your in-laws. But sometimes when the topic is sex, you can't control yourself and you might blurt out something at the wrong place and time. Then, instead of its leading to more sex, it leads to less.

If you're going to be having a conversation that involves intimate details about your life, be it your sex life or even financial matters, you have to choose carefully the locale for this talk. Having an intimate discussion at most restaurants, where other diners can hear what you say, make them far from ideal locales. The interior of a car can provide privacy, but if the subject matter is going to severely distract the driver, then it might not be the safest environment.

I usually recommend a walk down a quiet road or at a park. No one will be around, so you'll have plenty of privacy. There'll be a lovely setting to frame your words. And the act of walking can have a calming effect by burning off any adrenaline that talking about a touchy subject might create.

If you're going to have this talk at home, I wouldn't recommend the bedroom. That's the place where you most often have sex, and so talking there may imply that sex might ensue. If a request about a new sexual position is going to be rejected, it would be more awkward in this particular setting. Any other room would probably be fine.

Making Your Meaning Clear

I'm sure you've been in a conversation where one person meant one thing and the other person thought something else was meant entirely. If you weren't clear in the sexual arena, your partner might assume that you wanted to do something he or she would never do, such as anal sex, when in fact you just wanted to have vaginal intercourse from behind, doggie style, as it's called.

If your partner is reacting to what you propose in an unexpected or inappropriate manner, double-check to make sure that he or she really understood what you were saying. State your objective again clearly so that there's no chance miscommunication has occurred.

And if by chance you realize that there has been a miscommunication, my advice is to drop the subject, at least temporarily. If your partner is now upset because originally she or he didn't understand what you meant, then it's going to take a while for him or her to calm down. So the atmosphere won't be receptive to new ideas, and it would be better to table them.

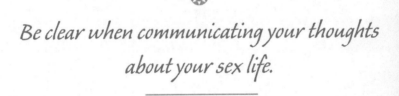

Be clear when communicating your thoughts about your sex life.

The Myth of the Silent Male

Some men pride themselves on being "a man of few words." While it's true that few words may come out of the mouths of such men, their brains are as active as anyone else's. So it's not that they don't have anything to say, but rather that they're tongue-tied. Such men are afraid that if they try to say what they feel, they'll be made fun of or be rejected.

As you might expect, any man who doesn't say much in general will have an even harder time talking when the subject matter is as touchy as sex. Not only won't such a man raise any sexual issues on his own, but if his partner does, he's likely to remain mum.

So while the strong, silent type does have opinions, he's going to have problems verbalizing them. One solution for the partner of a man whose cat has a firm hold of his tongue is to accept the risk of rejection and instead of bringing up a sexual desire verbally, to act physically. Let's say that over the years she's discovered that the only way she is able to have an orgasm is through oral sex. She meets a new partner, one of these men to whom a grunt is worth a thousand words and who certainly has no desire to talk about sex but to whom she is very attracted. She tries talking to him about her needs, but it seems as if she's not getting through. Well, she needs to physically lead his mouth where she wants it to go. (I'll leave the details of how to do that up to her.) Perhaps he'll turn away, and that will be somewhat painful. But to do nothing would mean not ever having orgasms, which isn't an acceptable situation. So rather than face having to leave him, or staying and never having orgasms, I recommend that she communicate her needs in a way that he is going to understand. Of course, she may end up concluding that dealing with such a man is too frustrating to be worth sticking around, but that's another story. But to the degree that he gives up his rights to voice his opinions, she must show the determination to lead them in the direction she believes they should be heading. And if you're already in a relationship with someone like this, it's never too late to instigate changes. So don't give up on getting your meaning across, but instead look for new ways to communicate.

Motor Mouths

Motor mouths, people who can't stop talking so that every thought that enters their heads pops out of their mouths milliseconds later, are a type that is not limited to women. After a while these continual torrents of words end up not being communicative. The partner of someone like this is going to just stop listening so that even if the motor mouth has something important to say, it's going to be difficult to get his or her message across.

In instances when there is something important to say, I might suggest using the written word to start the ball rolling. If it's the motor mouth who is doing the communicating, it's much more likely that her partner will pay attention to a written note. And if it's her partner, then he's more likely to get his message across than trying to elbow his way through the usual crowd of words coming from her.

Debaters and Passive Aggressive Partners

There are some people who will say the opposite of whatever you say, seemingly whether they agree with you or not. At some point in their life they discovered that they enjoy debating and so they use every opportunity for normal conversation to start a debate. But while they may be having a good time arguing, it makes it very difficult for anyone around them to make them understand what they are trying to say. Instead of listening, these debaters are only looking for ways to retort (which means they're not really listening to the message you are trying to convey).

Then there's the opposite type, the people who will agree with whatever you say, again whether or not they believe what they are saying at the time. You might label them passive aggressive because they'll say yes to a suggestion, but never actually do what they promised. They can be as frustrating to deal with as the debaters because when the conversation is over, you have no idea whether or not your message got through.

If you intend to stick it out with such a relationship, you have to recognize what is going on and respond forcefully. In both such instances, you have to tell your partner to stop putting up whichever front they've chosen and tell you how they really feel. And to show you how flexible I am, in these two instances I'm actually going to change some other advice I've given. With these types of people you might be better off having a conversation about sex in the bedroom and going right from the conversation into having sex. That might be the only way you're going to find out whether or not you got your message across. If, for example, the two of you have never used the 69 position, and you propose it, and then try to get your partner to engage in it with you, soon after you'll know where they stand, because either they'll do it or they won't. You may end up delighted with what occurs or disappointed, but at least you'll know what your mate really believes with regard to this specific proposal.

CASE HISTORY *Brian*

Brian came to see me specifically because he couldn't gather up the courage to speak to his wife about their sex life. She'd once made some grumbling comments, but at the time he'd pretended not to hear her, and ever since then, she hadn't said a word, nor were they having much sex. He told me that he wanted to speak to her about it, but he just couldn't do it. He said he got so nervous, fearing that he was going to hear the worst, that he'd walk out of the room.

Tips

So far I've been giving you some general advice on communicating with your partner, especially about sex. But what if you're like Brian and still can't manage on your own? Here are some tips that may help you.

We Need to Talk

Many people will go over and over in their head how a particular conversation is going to go, such as asking the boss for a raise or talking to a spouse about sex. Each time they do that, it raises the stakes and makes them more nervous. If you find yourself in this situation, what I recommend you do is just gather your courage up sufficiently to say, "We need to talk." Once those words are out of your mouth, your partner is going to want to know the nature of the subject and will help you carry the ball. So don't think about the entire conversation and what you're going to say. Just look toward opening the door. Once you get started, actually having the conversation will be a lot easier.

Seize the Opportunity

If you say to yourself, *I'm going to talk to my wife/husband in an hour*, for that hour you're going to get more and more nervous and by the time that hour has gone by, you may have lost your courage. But when the right moment comes along, you have to jump right in. If you're a male who wanted to ask your wife to engage in oral sex and she's eating an ice-cream cone, then just say to her, "You know, Dr. Ruth says that women should practice how to have oral sex by eating an ice-cream cone." Once you've opened the way, you'll have a lot easier time having that conversation. But such moments are often short, so you can't dillydally. Seize the opportunity as soon as it presents itself.

Use Cue Cards

Say you just can't spit out the words. You're so nervous that your mouth gets all dry and you can't force yourself to do it. Then try writing the appropriate phrase on a cue card, that is, a card or piece of paper of any size. If you're a woman who wants more foreplay, write down the words "more foreplay" and then hold up the card in front of your partner—at the appropriate moment, of course. He won't understand exactly why you're holding up this card, but you'll have succeeded in getting the conversation started in a way that neither of you can ignore.

Leave Notes

If you're so much of a scaredy-cat that you can't hold up a cue card, then put it in with his socks. When he goes to get a pair of socks, he'll see the card in your handwriting and he'll undoubtedly ask you about it. And bingo! The conversation will have started. (If he brings it up at a time you can't talk, then simply say, "It's something I want to talk to you about but not now.")

Use Humor

Sex is not inherently a serious topic, but people turn it into one. However, if you use humor to get your message across, that will be like giving a sugar-coated pill instead of one that tastes terrible. So if you know that you usually make love on Friday nights after the kids have gone to bed, go to the bathroom earlier and write in lipstick across your breasts, "More foreplay!" Yes, it will get the message across, but it will also be funny, so it might make it easier.

Get Help

If you walk into a card store these days, you'll find very creative cards on almost any topic. Even if you can't find one that's exactly right, you can probably find one that is both humorous and appropriate. Again, if you're having problems speaking, you need to get the ball rolling, and a card might do the trick.

Be High Tech

There are lots of new methods of technology around, so use them to help you. For example, when you're both home, use your cell phone to call your partner on your home phone. When he or she picks up, say "Is this a good moment to talk?" If you're shy, starting the conversation while you're in another room will make it easier, but then you can quickly get in closer contact to actually have the talk. Or if your partner is online, use the text message feature on your cell phone to send him or her the same message.

Use Subterfuge

I spoke about inertial forces before, how it's difficult to get an object moving if it's at a dead standstill. The same holds true for conversation. Going from not talking to talking about sex can be difficult. But what if you start the conversation about something else entirely. What if you say to your partner, "We need to talk about what to do about that leak in the garage roof." After you've had that discussion, then you can say, "There's something else I'd like to talk about" and that will have to do with sex. You'll see that if you're already talking, it will be a lot easier to make this segue than to start a conversation about sex from scratch.

Use Props

Let's say you want to talk about oral sex but you can't seem to find a way to get started. Since there's so much written about sex these days, I suggest you find an article, either in a publication or on the Web, and use that as a starting point for your conversation. If you were to say, "I just read in the paper that 42 percent of couples engage in oral sex regularly," that will certainly get a response from your partner. Then it will be easier to steer the conversation toward your own sex life.

As you can see, there are lots of ways to open a line of communication between you and your partner about a sexual issue. I hope these tips will make it a little easier for you, but the tips alone aren't enough; in the end it's up to you to open your mouth and start the conversation.

Don't avoid having a conversation about sex, but instead do whatever it takes to begin talking about your sex life.

Secret 9

Prepare for the
Changes That Lie Ahead

Change is inevitable. If your relationship has only been going on for a few months or even a few years, then the changes that have occurred may be so slight that you won't even notice them. But if you're in a long-term relationship, then there's no escaping the effects that the passing of time will cause, and this is definitely true when it comes to the differences that will occur in your sex life.

How much your sex life is going to change in any given period of time is going to depend on how old you are. The younger you are, the fewer changes there'll be, and those that do occur will be slight, but if you are in a certain age bracket, fifties to early sixties, you can expect more changes, some of which can threaten your sex life and even your relationship.

So when it comes to these changes you need to educate yourself in order to be prepared for the effects of aging on your sex life.

None of these changes need to threaten your relationship if you're forewarned of their arrival and know how to deal with them when they do occur. Where they are most damaging is when they blindside a couple. If a couple is taken unawares, then there's a good chance that they'll react in a negative way that can be very damaging, sufficiently so to completely destroy their relationship.

Early Changes

The sex life of all couples will cool down after a while. Certainly, they should do whatever they can to make sure that this cooling off doesn't get out of hand, but when one partner looks for outside causes, such as his or her partner having an affair when there's really no evidence to justify it beyond a minor change in their sex life, that's when any cooling down can cause serious relationship issues.

In the case of Tina and Jeb there was an added factor, the fear of the responsibilities of becoming a parent. That, too, is some-

---

CASE HISTORY *Tina and Jeb*

When Tina and Jeb were dating in college, they couldn't get enough of each other. They got married soon after graduation and their sex life continued to blossom. But after about a year, Tina noticed that Jeb wasn't as interested in having sex with her. They still had sex once or twice a week, but the intensity seemed to have disappeared. Then Tina went to an office party that Jeb's firm was having and met Jennie, the woman whose cubicle was next to Jeb's. She was stunning. Tina managed to have a one-on-one conversation with her, in which she learned that Jennie had broken up with her boyfriend about three months before. Then Jeb came up to them with a drink in his hand for Jennie. That night they had a terrible fight.

Tina assumed that the change in their sex life had grown out of an affair Jeb was having with Jennie. Now it's not that Jeb didn't appreciate Jennie's beauty; all the men at the firm were aware of her when she was close. But Jennie had nothing to do with Jeb's desire for Tina. No, the real problem was that Tina had dropped several hints that she wanted to have a baby. Jeb was not ready for fatherhood, and so that's what was making him shy away from having sex as often.

thing that many young couples face. And it can be worse when the woman is on the pill. In such instances, she's in control of preventing a pregnancy, and some men end up not trusting their partner to take the pill every day to protect themselves from parenthood, so they begin to avoid having sex. The best solution to that particular problem is for him to use condoms, an added measure of security that often will do the trick of reviving their sex life.

Babies

Babies are wonderful, but they usually play havoc with a couple's sex life, especially during the early months. Because they're afraid of hurting the baby, most expectant fathers don't mind giving up sex while their wife has a huge belly, though they actually can't. But while they're waiting for that belly to disappear, their goal is to get back the sex life they lost. Of course that's not likely to happen right away. New mothers are usually exhausted, and even when their doctor gives them the go-ahead to have sex, it's not necessarily their first priority.

My advice in such cases, after the doctor has given that go-ahead for sex, is for the new mother to plan on some times to have sex. Her libido may be overwhelmed by her new status, both emotionally and physically, but if she has sex, there's a good chance that she will become aroused and enjoy herself. At the very least, she'll be keeping her husband from being sexually frustrated. So rather than use the baby as an excuse, which is not good psychologically because the baby comes between the parents, it's better to find a way to jump-start your sex life.

If you're in a situation that is having a negative impact on your sex life, take the necessary steps to jump-start your sex drive.

CASE HISTORY *Blanche and Edward*

At the end of August, Blanche and Edward drove away from the college where they'd dropped off their last child and headed back to their now empty house. They were both sad to be leaving their daughter, but under normal circumstances that sadness might soon have turned to glee, since many parents in these circumstances find their love life blooms because of their newfound privacy. In this instance, however, sexual escapades were the last thing that were going to replace their daughter's presence. In fact, as they rode in total silence back home, it was a preview of what was to come.

Empty Nest Syndrome

The phrase *empty nest* can bring good news and bad news. When it's linked to the word *syndrome*, the connotation is most definitely negative. This combination indicates that the only ties holding the relationship together were the children. The couple at this point has nothing in common with each other and their only interaction for many years has been strictly limited to the subject of their kids. Once the children have flown the coop, the reality of their empty relationship sets in.

I see couples like this all the time and, sadly, there's not much I can do for them. The damage to their relationship is such that it's too late to make repairs. It's not like a tear that can be sewn together; instead, it's as if the relationship has been shredded. The time to fix empty nest syndrome isn't when the kids are gone, but long before they've left. Only preventative measures really work. All couples must take stock of their relationship and if they see that it is being eroded, they must begin taking action as soon as possible. All parents make sacrifices for their children, but they must not sacrifice their own relationship. That's asking too much.

They must do things together, including having sex but also going to the movies, having dinner with friends, taking vacations, and so forth, so that they remain a couple rather than two strangers raising a family.

CASE HISTORY *Sarah and Harvey*

Sarah and Harvey were in their late fifties. They were both aware that they'd been having sex with less and less frequency. They were also both aware that Harvey no longer became excited when he saw Sarah in the nude. Neither one said a word to the other about these changes. But they both had come to the same conclusion: Harvey was no longer attracted to his wife. Harvey's solution was to look at porn on the Internet and masturbate. Sarah suspected that he was having an affair and kept looking through his belongings in search of evidence. In poring over their credit card bills, she discovered a charge for a restaurant on a night he'd called to say he was working late. That was enough evidence for Sarah. She wanted a divorce. Harvey didn't quite remember what had happened that night, though eventually he realized that he and a coworker had gone out for dinner and then returned to their desks to complete a project. Luckily for them he and Sarah agreed to see a counselor, me, before unleashing their lawyers on each other.

Younger men have what is called a psychogenic erection. That's an erection that occurs spontaneously, without any physical stimulation. A man sees a picture of a naked girl, or his wife stepping out of the shower, and his penis jumps to attention. At a certain age, a man loses the ability to have psychogenic erections. There is no way to predict at what age this is going to occur for any individual man. Commonly it takes place in the late fifties or early sixties. But for men who are out of shape, it could happen in their forties.

By the way, this is the preerectile dysfunction stage. These men do not need Viagra or one of the other pills. They can still have erections; they just require physical stimulation to have them. In other words, like their wives, they now need foreplay. While I understand that no man is going to look at this as a positive turn of events (men are very vain about their erections), on the other hand, it is not a calamity either. But it can have serious consequences if both the man and his partner react the way Sarah and Harvey did. Or should I say, overreact.

Since the loss of the ability to have a psychogenic erection is a signal of circulatory problems, a man to whom this occurs long before it is supposed to happen shouldn't ignore the change but should go for a checkup and report what has happened to his doctor. And older men might say something to their physicians too because it could be a sign of the very early stages of a circulatory problem.

If Sarah and Harvey had known that this problem was on the horizon, and recognized it when it entered their bedroom, then it would have been only a blip in their sex life. But because they were caught unawares, this mild change got blown out of proportion and could have wrecked their marriage.

Menopausal Changes

The other change that couples in their fifties face is menopause. Obviously, only the woman undergoes menopause, but it does have an impact on both their sex lives. Many postmenopausal women secrete much less vaginal lubrication when they are aroused. If they have intercourse, it is painful. In fact, just inserting the man's penis into her vagina can be painful, if not impossible. The solution is simple; such couples need to use an artificial lubricant. If they don't, then sex will remain painful for her, and that will put an end to their sex life.

Because her natural lubrication was not only useful for preventing pain but was also a physical sign that she was sexually aroused, some men react negatively to this loss. They don't like having to ask their partner whether or not she is fully aroused, or may even assume that she can't be aroused if she's not lubricating. (And some women react similarly, not believing or repressing feelings of sexual arousal because they are no longer lubricating.)

While the physical changes of menopause do need to be accounted for by a couple, the cessation of a woman's cycle is not all bad news for their sex life. No longer having periods means that a couple who used to avoid that time of the month can now have sex any day they choose. And not having to worry about causing an unintended pregnancy can also give a psychological lift to a couple's sex life.

Erectile Dysfunction

I already told you that at a certain age men lose their ability to have psychogenic erections, but some men, not all, eventually lose the ability to have erections altogether. That's a condition referred to as erectile dysfunction, or ED. In some cases this is caused by a medical condition, like diabetes, but in many others it's a factor of the aging of the circulatory system. A man's erection is caused by blood flowing into the penis, but if his circulatory system has become weakened as he grows older, having a strong enough flow of blood into the penis becomes more difficult to achieve. That's when drugs like Viagra, Levitra, and Cialis come in. They work on the circulatory system, allowing a man to have an erection if he so desires. That's very important. They don't give a man an erection. He has to have the desire for it in order for that to happen. But since the advent of these pills, men who have sexual desire can have erections even if they suffer from ED.

Sorry to say, these pills aren't right for every man. Any man who has a heart problem will probably be told by his physician that he is not a candidate for these pills. In that case, there are other solutions. There are surgical procedures that can replace the spongy tissue in the penis with an inflatable system that he can pump up when he wants to have an erection. There have been tremendous improvements in these devices so that men who have them are quite pleased with the results.

CASE HISTORY *Ron and Emma*

Ron and Emma had been married for more than forty years. They'd had a very satisfying sex life early on, but as they both got older, it had started to dwindle. Emma wasn't so concerned about it, but when Ron began to have difficulty obtaining and maintaining his erections, he grew quite frustrated. Because he was one of those men who didn't like to go to doctors, he delayed going to his doctor to talk about it for several years, but eventually he gathered up his courage and made an appointment. His doctor gave him the all clear and a prescription, which Ron rushed to have filled.

Ron hadn't told his wife that he was going to the doctor and when he came home, he took one of the pills and a little while later surprised her by proudly showing her his penis in its erect state, a sight she hadn't seen in a while. Of course he wanted to try out his newly refurbished equipment, but the surprise appearance of his erect penis didn't have a positive effect on Emma's libido. In fact, it had the opposite effect, and she told him to "put it away" and leave her alone. Needless to say, this led to a series of arguments that threatened the marriage when Ron suggested that perhaps he should find someone else more interested in his new-found powers.

The problem that this couple faced is one that any couple whose sex life has diminished will encounter if the introduction of such a pill into their relationship is not carefully prepared. As we discussed earlier, communication regarding sexual matters is vital, so Ron should have told Emma what he planned on doing. It wasn't a question of giving her veto power but rather offering her the opportunity to get used to the idea that he wanted their sex life to start up again. And once he had a bottle of pills, he should have consulted with her when would be an appropriate time to take one.

While each case is going to be different, I would say that it would be appropriate for the man to woo his partner back into bed, even if that takes a few days. I know he's going to be impatient to try out the pill to see if it works as soon as he gets home, and perhaps if he's prepared the way ahead of time, that could happen; but the more patient he is with his partner in the beginning, the more that patience will pay off in the long run. If his partner feels that he's showing her the utmost respect and is in no way pressuring her to have sex, the more likely she will be to respond positively. But the more forced she feels, the less pleasure she'll get, and that will only reinforce her belief that sex is not an activity she wants to partake of and will cause more conflicts as time goes by.

If there has been quite a gap between the last time a couple had intercourse and the first time they do after he has taken one of these pills, the couple must not assume that their sex life is going to immediately go back to the way it was twenty years ago. She probably is now menopausal, and so lubrication will be needed. Older men sometimes take longer to ejaculate, and so the couple may need to apply the lubricant several times in order for her not to suffer any pain. In fact, I would recommend that if intercourse lasts too long that first time (which might be the result of nerves) the couple should stop and the woman should help the man have an orgasm in some other manner. If intercourse were to go on too long, to the point where she felt some discomfort, she might later feel reluctant to agree to a repeat performance. Also, the man should see to it that his partner has an orgasm so that they both share in the pleasure of this experience.

Health Issues

As people get older, they begin to run into more and more health issues. Some are annoying, some are life threatening, and many have an impact on a couple's sex life. And because there are two people aging at the same time, the odds of a couple encountering at least one health-related problem that has a negative impact on their sex life grow as they get older. I'm not going to cover the litany of potential health problems in this book. Instead I'm going to give you some general advice that will cover the effects of most of them. And the most important piece of advice I can offer is to speak to your doctor.

How to Talk to Your Doctor About Sex

As we've seen, people who have sex together are not always good at communicating about this subject. So it shouldn't come as a surprise that sexual functioning is not a topic that patients have an easy time talking to their physician about either. And since physicians are only human, most aren't very adept at raising this subject and so it often slides right by and the patient and his or her partner are left with a sex life that might no longer be functioning; not because it couldn't be but as a result of ignorance. Preventing that from happening is the secret this chapter discusses, but in some cases the educational process has to spread from the couple to their doctors. In other words, just because a doctor feels too uncomfortable to bring up the sexual ramifications of a health problem, or does so in only a perfunctory manner, it should not be allowed to ruin your sex life. In order to prevent this from occurring, you, the patient, must take the initiative.

Since talking about sex is a difficult topic, make it easier by writing down your questions ahead of time. This will help to make sure that you don't skip any, as these days a visit to a doctor's office always seems rushed. Having a cheat sheet will also make it easier to get the words out as you can phrase them in the most palatable form when you write them down. If it helps you, instead of asking them out loud, you could hand your physician the questions for him or her to read and then answer.

I wish I could promise you that your doctor will be able to solve every problem, but the truth is that the negative impact of some health issues on your sex life can't be fully solved. However, often there is a solution. For example, many medications may lower your libido, your desire for sex. On the other hand, there are usually several alternative drugs available that are equally effective at what they're supposed to do while causing much less of a negative effect on your sexual functioning. So if your doctor gives you permission to try another prescription, that may at least alleviate if not solve the problem.

Another issue that a doctor can help with is fear. This can be particularly damaging when one member of a couple has a heart condition. If one or both partners worry that sex might cause a heart attack, obviously this is going to put a damper on their sex life. But if a doctor gives the couple the all clear, then this fear can be alleviated. While cardiologists are supposed to raise the issue of sex after heart attacks, some either gloss over it, or skip the subject entirely, which is why I am telling you to raise this issue.

Impossible Obstacles

I once had as a guest on my television show a man who was a quadriplegic who had a wonderful sex life with his wife. Many seemingly impossible obstacles can be overcome if you have the right attitude.

Certainly many health issues pose a challenge to having sex, but most of these can be met if you work at it. And in my opinion, sex is too important, both to each of you as individuals as well as to your relationship, to give it up without putting up a fight. I have helped couples well into their eighties restart their sex life, so I know it's possible. And I also know that the rewards are well worth the effort. So never assume that your sex life is over just because some medical issue caused you to press the pause button for a time.

When the Problem Is Mental

So far it may appear that I have been talking only about physical disorders that can have a negative impact on your sex life, but certainly so can mental problems. And the biggest one in this category is depression. Even mild depression can eat away at your libido, and the medications used to help people who are depressed also tend to have the same effect.

While a depressed person may not feel the need to have sex, their partner ends up being doubly affected: not only must this person adopt the caregiver role, but her or his sex life is interrupted. The solution in cases where having sex together is not likely to happen in the near future is masturbation. I understand that it is not the ideal choice, but it's better than being sexually frustrated. If you're having to deal with caring for someone with any health-related issue, that's already going to make you a bit irritable. So for both your sake and your partner's, don't add to the stress of your lives by not doing anything about your sexual needs. For more information on masturbation, please see Chapter 10.

Self-Esteem Issues

As we grow older, our bodies change, and in most cases, not for the better, at least as that word is defined by Madison Avenue. We live in a culture that dotes on youth, and so most people do whatever they can to appear as youthful as possible, especially women. But since this is a battle you can never completely win, as the years creep by, your appearance will change.

This is usually a gradual process, so most people get used to their changing bodies, as do their partners. But sometimes the change is not so gradual, such as those caused by pregnancy or disease, such as breast cancer. And for some people, even the gradual changes are too much to bear.

CASE HISTORY *Bernie and Camille*

When Camille was a teenager, she had a perfect figure, and she loved the attention it drew when she would wear her bikini on the beach. But after she had children, she just couldn't seem to lose the weight she'd put on and her pride turned to shame. Bernie, her husband, actually thought that she had been a bit too skinny when they got married. Not only did he not mind the extra flesh that clung to her frame, but he found her more sexy than before. His problem was that Camille started doing all she could to hide her body from him. She always wore loose fitting clothes that hid her curves, and would change from her nightgown into street clothes in the bathroom, with the door locked. They did have sex together, but only under the covers. This was very frustrating to Bernie, who needed visual stimuli to become aroused. He tried over and over again to convince his wife that he found her very sexy and attractive, but his words couldn't inflate her own sense of self-esteem, which had sunk lower and lower.

Not only have I treated couples like Bernie and Camille, but I also get letters from men like Bernie all the time. These men don't understand why their compliments aren't enough to make their partners change their feelings about their bodies, at least in the privacy of their home. The reason, of course, is that problems of low self-esteem often stem from much broader issues than a few added pounds. More often than not, a person with low self-esteem needs to be treated by a therapist in order to get to the bottom of what is causing the outward symptoms and then help the person to overcome them.

While problems with low self-esteem can crop up at any time, they do tend to get worse as people's bodies show more and more signs of age. Luckily, if you're in a relationship that is a long-running one, you're both aging and so, hopefully, each of you can accept the changes in the other's appearance. And after a number of years, the strength of the relationship itself should more than make up for any added wrinkles or pounds.

While you can't stop the aging process, and I don't recommend plastic surgery and other medical intervention, I do strongly advise you, from the psychological viewpoint, to put up a fight. In other words, maintain or increase any exercise program that you've been following. Be careful of what you eat. What this does for you, and for your partner, is to show that you do care about your appearance and that whatever changes are occurring are not your fault. If you maintain a positive attitude, that will have a positive effect on your relationship and your sex life. Conversely, if you give up and say there's no point in fighting, then that will have a negative impact. So take action, not because you can stop the aging process, but because your positive outlook will do wonders for your relationship.

Secret 10

Mastering Masturbation

his book is supposed to be for couples, so you might think it strange that I've included an entire chapter on masturbation. There are two main reasons why I feel it is important to include this subject matter. The first is that masturbation does have a place within a relationship, but because of the many misconceptions around this activity, there's a lot of confusion about what its place should actually be. Second, despite having just told you that masturbation may be part of a relationship, it can also be abused.

Different Strokes

Some days when dinnertime rolls around you find yourself starving, while other days you're just not that interested in food. In other words, your appetite for food varies from day to day. The same is true with regard to your appetite for sex. Some days you crave it, but at other times the thought of having sex leaves you cold. The following is a letter, typical of the type I get all the time.

> My husband likes sex once in a great while. I would like it at least every other night. Plus I am very affectionate and he is not. How can I get him to want sex more and be more affectionate?
>
> I am 51 and he is 45. We've been married for 10 years. Please help.

Sometimes it's the woman complaining, sometimes the man, but the fact is that people's sexual appetites are all different. And they can differ from day to day, month to month, or year to year so that for a period of time one half of a couple might want more sex and then it's the other partner who feels the greater need.

There is nothing that I know of that can get two people to desire sex with the same frequency. There's no drug, vitamin regime, diet, or anything else that can work such a miracle. What every couple must do is find a compromise that works for them. And sometimes that compromise includes masturbation.

If two people have differing sexual appetites and one person masturbates in order not to become sexually frustrated, then there's absolutely nothing wrong with that. It's a very different situation if one person prefers to masturbate rather than have sex with his or her partner. That would mean that the partner of the masturbator would wind up sexually frustrated. But if masturbation is taking place only to increase the amount of sexual satisfaction for one partner, and doesn't take away from the other partner, then it's absolutely fine. So the secret about masturbation is:

Allow yourselves the freedom to masturbate as long as masturbation by one partner doesn't take anything away from the other.

Other Options

Of course there's nothing wrong with one partner offering sexual satisfaction to the other without also having an orgasm. That may be easier for women, who can just lie there while their partner satisfies himself. But men can also give a woman an orgasm using either their fingers, tongues, or a vibrator. The latter would be most appropriate if the reason that the man didn't want sex was because he was very tired, because using a vibrator would use the least amount of energy. The advantage of such sexual generosity is that it is a shared experience and can include other signs of affection like kissing or hugging. It is the preferable solution, but couples must realize it is not the only one.

CASE HISTORY *Mary and Phil*

Mary and Phil both worked for the same company, but different shifts. In some ways this arrangement helped them because it meant that their children would spend more time with a parent rather than a babysitter, and so the family also saved on child-care expenses. But having totally different schedules wasn't good for their love life, especially as some weeks one or both would also be working on a weekend.

Mary was so exhausted most of the time that she didn't really care that they weren't having sex more than once a month. But Phil needed the sexual release. Every once in a while Mary would allow Phil to wake her up and have a quickie, but more often than not, Phil would masturbate when he felt the need.

What brought them to see me was that Mary became very upset when she discovered that Phil was looking at some erotic DVDs when masturbating. They needed my help to heal the rift that had developed over this. Part of the reason that his method of masturbating was such a problem for Mary was that she felt guilty that she wasn't having sex with Phil more often, so she felt as if she were in actual competition with the women in the films while to Phil they were just a means to an end. He did become aroused by these women, but he wasn't emotionally attached to them in any way. And as he said in my office, he would have much pre-ferred to be having sex with his wife than masturbating, but the opportunities for sex just weren't there often enough.

It's sometimes called the "battle of the sexes" and one reason for these battles is sexual illiteracy; gaps in people's knowledge about human sexual functioning. In some instances the problems are caused by men not accepting something about how women function sexually and in others, such as the above example, the cause is a woman's unwillingness to accept how men function sexually. These battles are pointless because there's really no "solution" other than coming to an understanding about each other.

For example, women require clitoral stimulation to have an orgasm. It does no good for a man to ask why his wife can't have an orgasm during intercourse, as all those women in porn films seem to do. And men get aroused by visual stimuli to a much greater extent than do women, and for a woman to take this as a personal affront is foolish. Now I have often told men not to ogle other women when they are with their partner; that is bad manners. But for any woman to expect that her partner is not going to become aroused at the sight of some other sexy women is just not realistic. It's like getting mad at the sun for setting so early in the winter. You may not like that it gets dark so early but there's nothing you can do about it.

In the second half of this chapter I am going to discuss in greater detail the problems that can arise from masturbation, but for now, the point I want to get across is that if masturbation is appropriate within your relationship, then you have to allow your partner the freedom to masturbate in whatever manner he or she sees fit. If you are going to allow feelings of jealousy, be it for pictures or a vibrator, to develop, then your duty would be to find ways to increase the number of times you have sex with your partner. But that probably won't be a viable long-term solution, because then you might resent your partner for wanting sex so often. Therefore it is probably better to allow your partner the freedom to masturbate in whatever manner he or she sees fit.

Respecting Your Partner's Feelings

This freedom is a two-way street. Just as the partner masturbating may desire privacy, so might the partner who is not masturbating. In other words, whether or not the partner who masturbates should do so in front of his or her partner is a decision they have to make together. This is particularly true if one partner is masturbating while they are both in bed, keeping the other one awake. But even if that is not the case, there is no reason to show off that you are masturbating if it makes your partner feel uncomfortable. And to anyone reading this who objects and asks why they should be forced to masturbate in privacy if the reason they are masturbating in the first place is because their partner won't have sex with them, my answer is that if you are in a relationship it is supposed to mean that you love each other. And if you love someone, you should not want to make them feel bad. If your masturbation makes them feel uncomfortable, then do it in private. If what you require to masturbate, be it erotic materials or a vibrator or something else, also makes your partner feel uncomfortable, then you should not leave this material out where it is visible. On the other hand, the partner of someone who is masturbating shouldn't go sneaking around trying to find out their partner's technique, assuming that this masturbation is taking place in such a way as not to damage your mutual sex life.

Periodic Masturbation

In this discussion on masturbation, it might appear that this is a permanent state of affairs, but often that is not the case. Certainly many men turn to masturbation during the latter months of their partner's pregnancy if she doesn't feel up to having intercourse, as well as during that period right after birth when she is not able to have intercourse. And throughout a couple's life together there may be other times when masturbation may be particularly appropriate, such as if one partner has a long-term illness, or one has to go out of town for an extended period.

During such periods, the person masturbating shouldn't feel guilty, and the other partner shouldn't inquire about the possibility, either openly or privately. If one partner cannot provide sexual release to the other, then masturbation is not a negative activity, but a positive one, helping to maintain the relationship.

When Masturbation Gets out of Control

There is almost no activity that we humans do that can't be overdone. We all need to breathe, but it is possible to hyperventilate, which is dangerous. We all need to eat, but look at all the obese people around these days. And recent articles have shown that while no one running the marathon has suffered any ill effects from not drinking enough, some runners who drink too great a quantity of fluids during their run end up very ill, some even dying. And that's not to mention all the usual candidates for excess, such as alcohol, drugs, and gambling. And so it is with masturbation; some people masturbate too much.

I define too much masturbation in a relationship when one person masturbates rather than has sex with their willing partner, and the latter is left sexually frustrated. This is most definitely a problem, and potentially a very serious one.

CASE HISTORY *Greg and Joan*

Greg lost his job in the securities industry and just couldn't seem to get a new one. A year had passed and he was still out of work. But though he was the one staying home all day while his wife, Joan, went to work, he didn't feel that he should pick up any of the slack, so when Joan would come home in the evening, not only would dinner not be prepared, but there would be no food even to cook. On top of that, the house was messy and the laundry not done. Greg was willing to do "manly" chores, like repairing a leaky faucet, but he refused to do anything he felt was beneath him, especially at this period in his life when because he'd lost his role as the breadwinner, his sense of manhood was even more vulnerable. Needless to say, Joan was furious at him about this, but because she knew how bad he felt at not having a job, most of the time she didn't comment on it. But whenever Greg brought up the subject of sex, she let him know that she was too tired because of all the housework she had to do after coming home from work. Since Greg had all day with nothing much to do, he didn't really mind not having sex with his wife because he had plenty of opportunities to masturbate. But as they grew more distant sexually, the entire relationship became more and more strained.

The substitution of masturbation for mutual sex is not a new issue between married people, but up until recently the cause has been a problem in the relationship, as in the case above. If the two partners are not getting along, then one partner may prefer masturbation to sexual intimacy. And by the way, the partner masturbating might not always realize the source of the problem. Very often someone who doesn't feel like having sex with their partner doesn't see the underlying reason. For example, a young mother who feels that her husband isn't helping her enough with child care might not think that her loss of sexual desire is connected, and yet it is. But while that type of issue has been around for a long time, today we're seeing the sex life of couples deteriorating for a different reason.

Too Much Erotica

Recently I've received a lot of mail from women saying that their husbands have either drastically reduced the number of times they have sex or stopped altogether, and the cause is their partner's attraction to erotic material available on the Internet, though the problem is not a one-way street. I also hear from couples with Internet problems where chatting is the issue rather than erotic materials. In most of those cases, it is a woman who is the one ignoring her partner rather than the other way around.

The Internet has changed so many facets of our lives, it's not surprising that it would affect our sex lives. Adult sites attract the highest number of visitors. (The number of hits these sites are getting has dropped a bit recently, but they still lead the pack.) With all this sexual material so easily at hand, it's not surprising that some men would get tangled up in this particular web.

Two Lures

I believe there are two separate lures at work with regard to Internet porn. The first is the obvious one, that men like to look at images that arouse them, and there's no shortage of such material on the Web, much of it absolutely free. But I also think that there's another aspect to the process, and that's the element of hunting that's involved. After all, how can so many pictures of naked women hold so much appeal that a man would spend hours of his free time looking at them day after day? Yes, men like variety, but when you get into tens of thousands of pictures, then one breast really begins to look very much like the next. But with so many breasts, and every other body part available, what I think is occurring is that men are hunting for the sake of hunting. It would be easy enough to masturbate while looking at the very first naked woman and then shut down the computer. But if a man is going to spend an hour or two, then he's looking for something other than just an arousing image.

What is he looking for? It's probably something a little different for each man, but there are some basic categories we can assume are at work. Some men have, if not an actual fetish, then a strong attraction that comes close to being a fetish, for either a particular body part, like breasts, or for a particular type of woman, like Asian or plus-size women.

Some men have real fetishes—for example, for feet or women dressed in rubber. If his partner refuses to help him act out this fetish, then the man can satisfy it to some extent by looking on the Web.

Some men may be searching for women who look like an old girlfriend or perhaps an actual picture of that girlfriend. Or of a celebrity they fantasize about. Whatever it is they are looking for, it is this need to search that causes them to spend as much time on the Internet as the desire to actually look at naked women. The problem is that whatever the cause of their repetitive behavior, it can have a significant impact on their relationship with their partner.

As I said earlier, there is nothing wrong when one partner masturbates in order to relieve sexual stress because the other partner doesn't desire sex as often. But in the mail I get, the women (and sometimes men) are almost begging their partners to have sex but are getting turned down repeatedly in favor of masturbation while looking at erotica, or in the case of women, having cybersex via computer.

What makes the computer so insidious is that so much material is so easily available. Men initially bought magazines, and then brought home videos or DVDs, but the damage was somewhat limited. As I speculated before, I believe the computer is attracting these men in two ways; with erotic content, yes, but also with an environment in which to hunt down that content.

Men are hunters at heart and so there is an instinctual yearning for the chase. Erotic images in more limited numbers were available long before every home had a broadband connection, which is why I say that the sudden growth of this problem must be related to something other than just the need to look at erotica.

Why is this important? There are two reasons. The first is that many women resent it when their partner looks at images of naked women because they feel competitive. And the more their partner looks, and the more he prefers looking to having sex with her, the worse she feels. So what I want to get across is that a large part of the attraction that lures a man to surf the Web for hours night after night is not the sexual images themselves, but their sheer volume. When you buy a magazine, such as *Playboy,* and you flip through the pages and see whatever images of naked women are inside, that's it, you're done. And if a man could limit himself to one or two magazines a month, the problem of skipping sex with his partner would be minimized. But the Web offers infinite possibilities for searching. If there are millions of images available, and these sites keep adding to them every day, then it is impossible to look at them all. And so it becomes like a perpetual itch. Even the satisfaction of an orgasm after masturbation doesn't necessarily end the search. It's similar to the appeal of episodic television, and especially soap operas, where you keep coming back to see what happens next. And so it is not an individual woman that a wife is competing with, like Miss July, but it is closer to the lure of the golf course, to which a man returns again and again in order to see how he does. If it was easy to score a hole in one on every hole, the golf courses would be empty. It's the challenge that is the lure. And similarly, the vast quantity of sexual material on the Web poses another type of challenge, mixed in with a solid dose of sexual arousal, you can be sure.

The Cure

Obviously, marriages where the two partners are not having sex are not going to thrive, or in many cases even survive. At the same time, the Internet is not going to disappear. This pool of erotic material is probably here to stay. So how should couples who are having problems with this issue find a way out?

Let me begin by making a comparison. There are families that are ruined by alcohol, drugs, or gambling, yet you'll find alcohol in almost every home and the effects are, in most cases, neutral, or even positive when it comes to sex. There are some people who have what is called an addictive personality and when they run into a lure like alcohol, gambling, or porn, they find themselves hooked. And so some of the same methods used to alleviate these other addictions can be applied to an addiction to porn.

When a wife confronts her husband on an issue like this, in most cases his initial reaction will be to deny that he has any such problem. He'll do that out of guilt, not because he doesn't know that he has a problem. And if his wife is acting in an accusatory manner, in all likelihood he'll continue to deny it. Or else he'll promise to stop, but the first chance he gets, he'll go back to his old habit. So confrontation and anger are not part of the solution.

What I would suggest a wife do in such a situation is to say to her husband, "Honey, I love you a lot, but Internet porn is having a very negative impact on our sex life, our marriage, and on me. There's a simple way to stop this from continuing. I'm going to put a software filter on our computer that will prevent it from accepting material from these types of sites. I'm not going to look through every DVD or magazine in this house to see if it's pornographic, but I do want to put an end to porn entering the house through our computer."

As I said earlier, no two people have the same sexual appetite, so in this scenario, the wife is not telling her husband that he can never masturbate while looking at erotic images again. What she's suggesting is to cut off the source that turned masturbation into an addictive type of behavior.

I would not encourage this approach to become a discussion. I believe that in many cases, the husband is going to breathe a sigh of relief, at least inwardly. He's going to be happy that his wife is helping him to keep their marriage together, knowing that on his own he couldn't stop. In other cases, the husband is going to scream and shout and say to her that she better not try to stop their computer from accepting sexual material. If that happens, she should say, "Fine," drop the subject, and then contact a divorce lawyer. Perhaps when he receives the divorce papers, he'll have a change of heart, but if not, she'll be better off out of the marriage.

You'll notice that after telling you over and over in this book to get professional counseling, I did not advocate that in this instance. I'm certainly not against the concept of therapy, and would say that if the wife wanted to see a therapist to help her get through this tough period in her life, she should do so. But if a man, or woman, has a problem that is that severe, I don't think counseling is going to work, at least not at this stage in their relationship. Perhaps when he's faced with ending his marriage, he might bring up the idea of seeing a counselor or agree to go if his wife held such an option out to him. But I think in some instances it will take being at the edge of the precipice to get such men to grab on to this option, as happens with many alcoholics and compulsive gamblers. And I certainly don't think that his wife should fight over this issue any longer because the only results will be high blood pressure and other negative health effects.

"But what if there are children," I hear some of you saying. "Is having sex so important that divorce is the only option?" If this were just about sex, I would have to say no. If a woman's husband had an accident and couldn't have sex any longer, I would never suggest that she leave him. If it's just a matter of sexual frustration, she can always turn to masturbation. But this particular behavior isn't just about sex. A husband who's spending hours looking at Internet porn is most likely not being a loving husband in other ways because he's going to feel that if he hugs and kisses his wife, she's going to want to have sex, which he can't deliver. What this habit will already have done, and will continue to do, is pull them apart emotionally.

And being in a marriage without any emotional content, without any love, is not healthy, whether or not there are children involved. You have only one life, and you shouldn't live it in misery for the sake of your children.

The Distaff Side

And what happens if it's a woman who can't stop herself from chatting with one or more men? Does chatting, even if it does not involve so-called cybersex, do serious damage to the couple's emotional life?

I get many people asking me whether or not such chatting is "cheating." If someone is chatting with another person for whom they've developed a strong emotional bond, then I say it is cheating. If someone is chatting with people about this or that subject that they share an interest in, like collecting antique dolls, and there is no emotional bond but it does take up a lot of their free time, then it is no worse than spending too much time watching TV or playing golf or pursuing any other activity that takes you away from your partner. These are situations that you should be able to handle via communications and compromise. If you can't, then this type of situation could signify a relationship problem, for example, if one partner didn't want to spend time with the other. But if it's just a question of needing to spend more time together in order for the relationship to be healthy, then the couple needs to figure out how to handle the situation. (Ideally they could develop mutual interests that they could pursue together.) But if the chatting is with one person and of a very personal nature, then that's a much more serious problem.

Here again, the Internet has changed the way we live. Before the Internet, having a long-term emotional relationship without physical contact was just not that common. If you did have a good "friend" of the opposite sex, you'd have to see each other to communicate, and so the relationship would eventually turn physical. So since it would turn physical, there was no doubt that it was cheating, and that would keep most people from going down that path to begin with. But by chatting over the Internet, you can create emotional bonds with someone who might live clear across the country. While some of these affairs do turn physical, most do not, but they still tear at the fabric of a marriage. If one half of a couple is emotionally involved with someone else, that couple's relationship can't be considered to be on solid ground. But because it doesn't fit the description of cheating, it's easier to miss the exit sign when it's time to stop going down this particular road.

And then some of these cyber-relationships do end up having a physical component, though rather than intercourse, it's masturbation. But at that point, the effect is no different than if the

person is masturbating while looking at erotica, because if someone is sexually satisfying themselves via masturbation, they won't
be drawn to having sex with their partner.

So chatting can present the same dangers to a relationship as
looking at pornography, and it may be harder to deal with because
there's no software against it. The best thing to do would be to
unplug the computer or cancel your subscription to the Internet.
And again, if the person just won't stop, then rather than continue
in a relationship which is slowly heading downhill, the best thing
to do is to make plans to get out of it altogether.

When Masturbation Is the Only Way

Some people cannot get sexual satisfaction unless they masturbate. When this occurs in men, it's mostly a matter of habit. They
developed some individualized method of masturbation, probably
while frequently masturbating when they were younger, and then
when they do find a partner, they discover that they cannot climax
unless they masturbate themselves following the exact same pat-
tern that they've become used to using. When this develops in
women, it's often an issue of concentration. Having someone else
touch her, or even just be in the room, can spoil her concentration
to the point where reaching an orgasm is impossible.

Sometimes a sex therapist can help someone like this. And
sometimes help is not available. Obviously a sex life where one
partner can only climax via masturbation is not the most satisfying. But I'm one of those who believes that sometimes it's best to
look at the glass as half full. If every other aspect of a relationship
is good, then I would hope that a couple would not allow this one
aspect to pull the entire relationship down. Certainly the partner who can have orgasms via sex should be given those orgasms.
Then the partner who needs to masturbate can have an orgasm
afterward. The bottom line is that both partners can be sexually
satisfied throughout the relationship, and that's no small thing.

Conclusion

When you buy the latest must-have piece of electronic equipment, it always comes with an instruction booklet. It may not be entirely understandable, but at least there's some information to help you get started. But when it comes to your sexual relationship, the operation of which can be infinitely trickier than programming a DVR, there is no instruction manual. Most people try to figure out what to do on their own, and whenever you rely on the hit-or-miss approach, it's only natural to run into difficulties.

People like myself have devoted their lives to filling in that gap, and I guess the need for the services of sex therapists will never go away. In part that's because the attraction of sex is so strong, similar to the attraction of starting up that new electronic toy, that a lot of people rush into it without first learning the basics. Because of their haste, far too many couples never learn how to get the most of their sexual relationship, and in many cases, don't even get the least from it.

I hope you won't need to drop in on your local neighborhood sex therapist, especially after reading, and heeding, all the secrets I've given you in this book, but let's face it, it's not an impossibility. I'm sure you don't hesitate to go to your doctor or dentist when you run into some physical problem, so you shouldn't feel any different about contacting a sex therapist if you're having difficulties in that aspect of your life.

One question that stumps many people when it dawns on them that they do need professional guidance is how to find the right therapist. Certainly you can ask your doctor for a recommendation. Or if there's a large teaching hospital nearby, their department of social services will be able to make recommendations. Or else you can contact organizations that represent the people in the field. Below you'll find some listings that should be helpful to you

AASECT (American Association of Sexuality Educators,
  Counselors and Therapists)
P.O. Box 1960
Ashland, VA 23005
804/752-0026
www.aasect.org

American Academy of Clinical Sexologists
3203 Lawton Road, Suite 170
Orlando, FL 32803
407/645-1641
www.esextherapy.com

American Association for Marriage and Family Therapy
112 South Alfred Street
Alexandria, VA 22314
703/838-9808
www.aamft.org

American Psychological Association
750 First Street, NE
Washington, DC 20002
800/374-2721
www.apa.org

About the Authors

*D*r. *Ruth K. Westheimer* is a psychosexual therapist who pioneered the field of media therapy. She teaches at Yale University, where she is a fellow at Calhoun College, and Princeton University, where she is a fellow at Butler College; she is also an adjunct professor at NYU and a fellow of the New York Academy of Medicine. She has a private practice in New York and lectures worldwide.

Dr. Westheimer is the author of thirty-four books and has her own Web site (www.drruth.com). She has two children and four grandchildren, and resides in New York City.

Pierre A. Lehu has been Dr. Westheimer's "minister of communications" for twenty-seven years. This is the fourteenth book on which he has collaborated with her. He lives in New York, is married, and has two children.

Also by Dr. Ruth

SEX FOR DUMMIES
3rd Edition

Dr. Ruth K. Westheimer
with Pierre A. Lehu

Paperback
ISBN: 978-0-470-04523-7

"Her name and the distinctive thrill of her voice have become inextricably linked with the subject of sex."
—*New York Times*

"Dr. Ruth writes the way she talks — enthusiastically, nonjudgmentally, and informatively. . . ."
—*Booklist*

"Her energy level is higher than that of a charged particle."
—*People Magazine*

The bestselling guide to a rewarding sex life and a deeper relationship

Looking for the straight facts on sex? In this friendly, authoritative guide, renowned sex therapist Dr. Ruth gives you the latest on everything from oral sex and popular positions to new methods of birth control. She also debunks sex myths and covers new therapies to manage low libido, overcome sexual dysfunction, and enhance pleasure.

Discover how to

- Enjoy the first time
- Enhance foreplay and afterplay with your partner
- Avoid STDs and have safer sex
- Discuss sex with your kids
- Navigate cybersex

Other Books of Interest

THE SECRETS OF
HAPPILY MARRIED MEN
Eight Ways to Win Your Wife's Heart Forever

Scott Haltzman, M.D.
with Theresa Foy DiGeronimo

Paperback
ISBN: 978-0-7879-9414-3

"The insights in this book reveal a new and effective way for men and women to understand and appreciate each other. It shows what it really takes to create a loving and lasting relationship."
—John Gray, author, *Men Are from Mars, Women Are from Venus*

Dr. Scott Haltzman's insight for improving relationships is based on a man's special and unique skills, strengths, and powers. He has elucidated eight techniques to build a successful relationship. Each point is supported with specific analysis, guidelines and techniques based on male biology, neuro-science, brain differences, unique developmental stages throughout life and illustrated with true anecdotes from his website for married men, **www.SecretsOfMarriedMen.com**.

For a lasting commitment, a continuing guide to solving inevitable problems and bumps in the road, for more fun, better sex, genuine intimacy, and a life-long partnership—this dynamic book shows the way in a manner that finally includes an authentic male perspective.

DR. SCOTT HALTZMAN is clinical assistant professor of psychiatry and human behavior at Brown University, and medical director of NRI Community Services in Rhode Island. He also has an active private practice, with a focus on marriage counseling for individuals and couples. You can reach him at DrHaltzman@SecretsofMarriedMen.com.

THERESA FOY DIGERONIMO is the author of more than thirty-five books in the fields of education and parenting.

Other Books of Interest

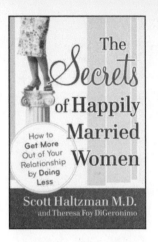

THE SECRETS OF HAPPILY MARRIED WOMEN
How to Get More Out of Your Relationship by Doing Less

Scott Haltzman, M.D.
with Theresa Foy DiGeronimo

Paperback
ISBN: 978-0-470-40180-4

"What a relief to read a book that makes so much sense. Scott Haltzman and his coauthor, Theresa Foy DiGeronimo's, keen insight into male and female differences and insightful counsel about how to create marital happiness should be read by all couples who want a formula for a passionate marriage. I heartily recommend this book to both men and women."
—Harville Hendrix, author, *Getting the Love You Want: A Guide for Couples and Receiving Love*

"If you're a married woman, buy this book. Haltzman not only understands men, he 'gets' women too; he's bilingual. He'll help you understand why the things you do to get through to your husband don't always work and more importantly, what you can do differently to get better results. His concrete, field-tested, and practical tips will, without question, make your husband, your marriage, and you happier and grateful you followed his advice."
—Michele Weiner-Davis, author, *Divorce Busting* and *Getting Through to the Man You Love*

From the authors of the best-selling *The Secrets of Happily Married Men* comes the much-anticipated ***The Secrets of Happily Married Women***.

Dr. Haltzman reveals his proven method for improving loving relationships in a humorous and entertaining style. His insight is drawn from his clinical practice and the thousands of contributors to his Web site, **HappilyMarriedWomen.com**. All techniques are supported with specific analyses and guidelines based on biology, neuroscience, brain differences, and unique developmental stages from youth to seniority. In addition, *The Secrets of Happily Married Women* contains compelling true stories, anecdotes, and confessions written by and for women (and the men who love them).